Cobwebs to Catch Flies

COBWEBS TO CATCH FLIES

Illustrated Books for the Nursery and Schoolroom 1700–1900

He who ne'er learns his ABC
For ever will a blockhead be:
But he who to his book's inclin'd
Will soon a golden treasure find

Joyce Irene Whalley

UNIVERSITY OF CALIFORNIA PRESS

Berkeley and Los Angeles 1975

For Peter and Alyson,
Melissa and Kenneth-Wynne

Frontispiece: Frontispiece to *Fables in
Monosyllables* [etc.] by Mrs Teachwell.
J. Marshall [1783].

UNIVERSITY OF CALIFORNIA PRESS

Berkeley and Los Angeles, California

ISBN 0–520–02931–3
Library of Congress Catalog Card Number: 74–27298

Printed in England

Contents

Preface

This work is to some extent a picture book about books with pictures; about teaching books but not text books. It is a study of the illustrated educational books which were used to instruct children during their earliest years, in the home rather than the school. It covers a period of about two hundred years up to the end of the nineteenth century, by which time the effect of universal primary education can be traced in the many different types of reading matter offered to the juvenile public.

Books do not exist in a vacuum but are shaped by the world around them; this is particularly true of those books intended to instruct the young. Past attitudes to children, to the natural world, to ethics and God, to foreigners and servants – there is plenty of social history to be gleaned from looking at early children's books. The choice of quotations and illustrations will, I hope, help to convey something of the atmosphere of the two centuries before 1900. The emphasis is on aspects of the books themselves, rather than on any educational theories they may propound, and the approach should appeal more to the general reader, art historian or bibliophile than the professional educationalist.

It is obvious that a book of this size, aimed at the general reader, cannot do more than reveal a portion of the vast amount of existing material. The subject of each chapter is itself worthy of a book and I hope that from my small beginnings others will produce works of greater depth within their own specialist field. Notes in the text have been kept to a minimum but, for the benefit of students of early children's books, a short bibliography and lists of books appropriate to the various chapters have been included, together with an index of publishers. It is helpful to know where copies of the books mentioned are to be found; all of them, except where specifically stated, are in the National Art Library, Victoria and Albert Museum, London. This Library already has a collection of over 5,000 children's books, and it is being augmented over a period of years by the generous gift to the nation of about 45,000 items from the collection of Anne and F. G. Renier.

Throughout our period, in the English-speaking world books crossed the ocean in both directions, and the same works were read and appreciated on each side of the Atlantic. Therefore, although many of the books discussed and illustrated here were published in England, they could in many cases be equally well reproduced with an American imprint. Sometimes the books were altered to suit the particular market, occasionally with no more than a change of publisher and place on the title-page. It was certainly not a one-way traffic; in the eighteenth century English children's books frequently appeared in the States with little or no change while, in the nineteenth century, many American children's books were published in England for the British market. Children's books on the continent of Europe followed a rather different pattern from their Anglo-Saxon counterparts, but there were many meeting points along the line and many favourites from the children's literature of various countries were also translated into other languages. I have therefore taken this opportunity to compare and contrast English and American children's books with their French and German contemporaries, whenever this seemed appropriate.

This book is mainly about instructional works, so it contains only part of the story of children's reading. The information given must be supplemented by reading literature from the other worlds of fairy tale, poetry and juvenile fiction. However, many works written for children, and not intentionally didactic, appear to the modern reader to continue the moral, religious and even instructional ideas of their time into a wider sphere. For this reason we can include such works as *Struwwelpeter* and even *Alice*, though, for the most part, examples have been chosen from less familiar works. Some readers may regret the omission of their own favourites, but I have in the main endeavoured to bring forward other, long-forgotten books and, through them, to recreate a past world of childhood.

Joyce Irene Whalley
London, 1974

Notes on the illustrations

The size of a book is given in centimetres, to the nearest centimetre. The place of publication is given only when it is *not* London. The dates given in the captions and in the text are not necessarily those of the first edition of the work; unless otherwise stated the date given is that of the copy illustrated or referred to.

Acknowledgements

Anyone writing on the history of children's books is conscious of the debt owed to predecessors in the field. In a study of this sort Harvey Darton's *Children's books in England: five centuries of social life* (2ed 1958) has been especially valuable; every re-reading of this pioneer work stimulates further thought. Other books which have been of considerable assistance are those by Mary Thwaite, Percy Muir, Muriel Jaeger and L. F. Field, details of which will be found in the bibliography. For American books, the works of A. M. Earle and A. S. W. Rosenbach have been invaluable and even more so, the recently published *Bibliography* of D'Alté Welch. Equally important has been the opportunity of talking and listening to such experts as Anne and F. G. Renier, who kindly read much of the first draft of my manuscript, and Iona and Peter Opie.

I am also greatly indebted to my colleagues who read or advised on the text: Vera Kaden, Anne Hobbs and Anthony Burton; also to Wynne Bartlett and my sister-in-law, Mary Whalley, who nobly proof-read for me, not once but many times. I should also like to express my appreciation of the photographic work of my colleagues Peter Macdonald and Stanley Eost, who often confronted the most unpromising material; also to thank Helen Angus for endlessly fetching and carrying all the children's books themselves for me. For much of the American material, especially for arranging photography of the various items, I wish to thank Virginia Haviland of the Children's Book Section, Library of Congress, and Frank M. Halpern of the Rare Books Department, Free Library of Philadelphia. I should also like to record my thanks to Miss Moira Johnston of Paul Elek Ltd. for the interest she has shown at all stages of the work and for her detailed care of all its aspects. Lastly I should like to pay tribute to my relatives and friends for their patience with me during my years of preoccupation with this book. I alone am responsible for any errors in it and for all opinions expressed therein.

The author and publishers gratefully acknowledge the following sources of illustration:

American Antiquarian Society: 2, 3, 16, 22, 55, 60, 68, 84, 154.

Library of Congress, Washington: 5, 93, 95, 99.

Rare Book Department, Free Library of Philadelphia: 1, 32, 47, 69, 82, 83, 88, 122.

Victoria and Albert Museum: 4, 6, 7, 8, 9, 10, 11, 12, 13, 14, 15, 17, 18, 19, 20, 21, 23, 24, 25, 26, 27, 28, 29, 30, 31, 33, 34, 35, 36, 37, 38, 39, 40, 41, 42, 43, 44, 45, 46, 48, 49, 50, 51, 52, 53, 54, 56, 57, 58, 59, 61, 62, 63, 64, 65, 66, 67, 70, 71, 72, 73, 74, 75, 76, 77, 78, 79, 80, 81, 85, 86, 87, 89, 90, 91, 92, 94, 96, 97, 98, 100, 101, 102, 103, 104, 105, 106, 107, 108, 109, 110, 111, 112, 113, 114, 115, 116, 117, 118, 119, 120, 121, 123, 124, 125, 126, 127, 128, 129, 130, 131, 132, 133, 134, 135, 136, 137, 138, 139, 141, 142, 143, 144, 145, 146, 147, 148, 149, 150, 151, 152, 153.

Introduction

During the Middle Ages formal education was unknown for most European children. Its place was taken by training for adult life, a state of affairs that, for the working-class child, continued well into the nineteenth century. In the medieval period the teaching of reading and writing was in the hands of the clergy and the language of instruction was the universal one of Latin.

In England, by the middle of the fourteenth century English was gradually beginning to supersede French in the speech of the upper classes, but it was the growth of trade and commerce and the rise of a middle class which made obvious the need for secular education in the vernacular. When all books were hand-written and learning was mostly by rote, education was necessarily limited. But the invention of printing in the middle of the fifteenth century, and the increased importance of a secular, middle-class influence, helped to pave the way for a much wider spread of education in the sixteenth century. Though Latin never lost its supremacy for those intended for the church or for a professional career, the curriculum widened before the practical needs of the community and the spirit of humanism.

The earliest books for children could be divided into two kinds: those that taught language and those that taught behaviour. The division reflected the different futures ahead of the children concerned. For the child whose expectations lay in the professional or clerical field (and for much of the Middle Ages these were one and the same), the 'primer' was the most important book. From this he learned his earliest Latin and his devotions. Chaucer's small choirboy 'lerned in that scole yeer by yere ... to singen and to rede. ... As he sat ... at his prymer'.[1] But what he learned 'to singen and to rede' was entirely of a religious nature. His noble contemporary might never master reading, even in his own language, with any facility, but he would be well exercised in his duty to his superior and in social behaviour. For him were compiled in the fifteenth century such works as *Stans Puer ad Mensam* and *The Babees Book*, which taught him all it was considered necessary for the well-born medieval child to know.

In England the secularization of education was further accelerated by the dissolution of the monasteries in the reign of Henry VIII, and this, together with the multiplicity of books consequent upon the spread of printing, and the influence of humanistic studies, completely changed the educational outlook. But, after the first impact of Renaissance learning had spent itself, there came a certain narrowing of the intellectual field with the rise of Puritanism towards the end of Queen Elizabeth's reign; not that Puritanism was itself inimical to learning, the scholarship of such as John Milton must refute that, but the emphasis changed. For the devout Protestant the study of the Bible was the best way to achieve the salvation of the soul, which to Catholic and Protestant alike was of primary importance. In Europe the effect of the Counter-Reformation was also reflected in religious

---

[1] 'The Prioresses Tale' from *The Canterbury Tales*, 1386–c. 1400.

LEAVING ENGLAND.

Our Pilgrim fathers left their home
  At persecutions nod,
More free in other lands to roam,
  More free to worship GOD.—

They crossed the broad atlantic wave,
  Their hapless babes beside them,—
Their trust in *one*, whose power could save,
  Should sorrow e'er betide them.

LANDING at PLYMOUTH.

Where now the town of Plymouth stands,
  On cold New England's coast,
A rock received the Pilgrim bands,
  Amid an Indian host.

Week after week by tempest borne
  Across a stormy sea,—
On shore they joyous hailed the morn,
  And bent to GOD the knee.

1 THE PILGRIMS; OR, FIRST SETTLERS OF NEW ENGLAND. Baltimore, F. Lucas, Jr; Philadelphia, Ash & Mason, 1825. A book engraved throughout and printed on one side of the page only, whose style should be compared with that of Belch's *William IV* (plate 65). The Pilgrims are clearly distinguished by their tall Puritan hats, which they wear in every illustration.

education. It is at this point that we make our first contact with the subject of the present book. The young child, conceived in sin and naturally evil, stood most in need of the attention of those concerned for the welfare of souls. It was from this source therefore, that the earliest books written specifically for children 'out of school' originate.

Having very briefly reached the middle of the seventeenth century and the beginning of books for children (somehow it does not seem quite right to call them 'children's books'), it is an appropriate moment to consider various general aspects of books for young people. Even today, when children's bookshops are increasing in number, the majority of children's books are bought by adults, and they are certainly almost always written by adults. This was also true in past centuries, and it was not surprising that then as now it was largely the adult world that was reflected in children's books. The books that were bought were those the grown-up thought the child *should* read; later, towards the end of the nineteenth century, that sentence could be modified to 'what the grown-up thought the child would *like* to read'. For the purposes of this book 'should' is perhaps more important than 'like'. To 'like' or 'enjoy' reading is a comparatively recent concept; it was unthinkable to many of our ancestors that so precious a gift as reading should be used for mere pleasure. Such an attitude inevitably affected those who governed the reading of children and, by implication, the whole relation of the adult to the child and to childhood. Even since the last war there has been a spectacular change in attitudes to children and in the behaviour of young people; how much greater must be the change between the attitudes of today and those of a hundred years ago – or of two hundred years ago? While surveying the development of books for children, it is therefore also necessary to consider changing attitudes to childhood over the same period.

For centuries there was very little concern to regard the child in any way that was special. With the Reformation the more extreme forms of Protestantism showed the greatest attention to Biblical learning on the part of the young, and it was this aspect of study which was most pronounced in the adult's attitude to the child and his reading; this was so both in Britain and in America, where many of those dissenting from the Anglican Settlement had taken refuge. The most important single subject of reading was religion; the religious controversies consequent upon the Reformation led, in both the sixteenth and seventeenth centuries, to a considerable amount of writing concentrated on religious topics. These were often closely linked with politics, especially in England, where the sovereign was head of the church, and heresy was also treason. The Puritans were particularly literate and from their aims and aspirations for the instruction of the young the earliest children's books originated. Since it was this same Puritan element that was predominant in the first settlers on the North American shores, it was not surprising that the earliest American books for children were those that emphasized the more important aspects of the Puritan tradition – Boston, a Puritan stronghold, produced the earliest American books for children. A firm belief in the rightness of their religious beliefs was passed on to the next generation and so helped to mould the future of their new land.

In both England and America during the centuries under consideration in this book, families were large; but infant mortality was high and the number of children surviving in any one family was usually small, many infants dying before they were five years old. It was an accepted fact of life, and even the most loving parent would see the wisdom of not wasting too much attention on a child who might not live to benefit. There was every inducement to limit the time of the difficult and dangerous period of youth, but those who survived must be able to take their place fully qualified in the adult world. There was no concept of childhood as we know it, no period of prolonged playtime or adolescence. The child was regarded as a small adult, clothed like one, and in many cases treated like one, and the sooner he behaved like one the simpler life would be for him. But living or, even more important, dying, a significant part of his existence would be taken up by his religious instruction. Text books apart, the first children's books were aimed at saving the soul from hell, a necessity which continued until well into the nineteenth century. As Darton has said,[1] seventeenth-century books for children, by writers such as Janeway, were meant to give pleasure and make the child happy – it was just that the writer's idea of happiness for children was so different from our own, or possibly the children's. The fear of hell was made very real and in some cases it is obvious that the young became neurotically obsessed with their souls; on the other hand with death frequently before them in their own families, the day of judgment must have seemed far more imminent than to the modern child.

Fortunately, at the beginning of the eighteenth century, there came a lightening of the harsh Puritan fare of children's literature. In 1715 Isaac

[1] *Children's books in England: five centuries of social life*, by F. J. H. Darton, Chap. IV, 1958.

Top:
2 DIVINE AND MORAL SONGS FOR
CHILDREN by Isaac Watts. Worcester,
Massachusetts, Isaiah Thomas, 1788.
11 cm. One of the most popular
books for English-speaking children,
constantly reprinted in both England
and America. This woodcut
illustration accompanies the poem
later parodied by Lewis Carroll as
'Twas the voice of the Lobster' in
Alice in Wonderland.

Bottom:
3 THE MOST SURPRISING ADVENTURES
AND WONDERFUL LIFE OF ROBINSON
CRUSOE, OF YORK, MARINER [by
D. Defoe]. Portland, Maine,
Thomas B. Wait, 1789. 15.5 cm.
An adult work early adopted by
children, particularly at a time
when the children's book market was
undeveloped. *Robinson Crusoe* has
always been popular in English-
speaking countries; it has also been
widely imitated, especially in
Europe.

I. *The* SLUGGARD.

'TIS the Voice of the Sluggard; I
heard him complain,
"You have wak'd me too foon, I muft
flumber again."

As the Door on its Hinges, fo he on his
Bed,
Turns his Sides and his Shoulders and
his heavy Head.

"A little more Sleep, and a little more
Slumber;"
Thus he waftes half his Days and his
Hours without Number;
And when he gets up he fits folding his
Hands,
Or walks about faunt'ring, or trifling he
ftands.

I pafs'd by his Garden, and faw the wild
Brier,
The Thorn and the Thiftle grow broader
and higher;

THE MOST SURPRISING
ADVENTURES,
AND WONDERFUL
LIFE
OF
Robinfon Crufoe,
OF YORK, MARINER.

CONTAINING

A FULL AND PARTICULAR ACCOUNT HOW HIS
SHIP WAS LOST IN A STORM, AND ALL HIS
COMPANIONS WERE DROWNED, AND HE ONLY
WAS CAST UPON THE SHORE BY THE WRECK;
AND HOW HE LIVED EIGHT AND TWENTY
YEARS IN AN UNINHABITED ISLAND, ON THE
COAST OF AMERICA, &c.

WITH

A TRUE RELATION HOW HE WAS AT LAST MI-
RACULOUSLY PRESERVED BY PIRATES,
&c. &c. &c.
[Daniel Defoe]

PORTLAND;
PRINTED AND SOLD BY THOMAS B. WAIT.
MDCCLXXXIX.
1789

Watts published *Divine Songs Attempted in Easy Language for the Use of* 2
Children. While still keeping the required moral and religious intent, Watts
wrote his 'songs' in simple words with simple verse forms, and showed a
sympathetic understanding of childish failings; moreover, he based his
examples on the everyday world of the child's experience; the family
squabbles, the busy bee, the whole world of home, street and field. He
appreciated that children were not the same as adults, and that the reading
matter intended for them, of whatever sort, should be adapted to their
capacities. But there was as yet little conception of the requirements of
different ages of children. Watts's songs were staple nursery fare for more

than 150 years and when, in 1866, Lewis Carroll chose to parody two of
them in *Alice's Adventures in Wonderland*, he could do so secure in the
knowledge that every reading child would be familiar with the originals.

But although at the beginning of the eighteenth century there was nothing
written for the child that he might read for pure pleasure, two works were
about to be published which would soon pass into the juvenile repertory.
These were *Robinson Crusoe* (1719) and *Gulliver's Travels* (1726). Owing to the
lack of children's reading, these books, though originally written for adults,
were soon adopted by the nursery, as *The Pilgrim's Progress* had been earlier.
Versions of them also appeared in popular chapbook form, joining the
substratum of literature, whence at a later date, with a change in reading
patterns, would re-emerge the traditional tales and nursery rhymes.

But the outlook for juvenile literature was about to improve for in 1744
the bookseller and publisher John Newbery, now established in St Paul's
Churchyard, London, issued *A Little Pretty Pocket-Book, Intended for the
Instruction and Amusement of Little Master Tommy and Pretty Miss Polly, with an
Agreeable Letter to Read from Jack the Giant Killer, as also a Ball and a Pincushion,
the Use of Which Will Infallibly make Tommy a Good Boy and Polly a Good Girl*.
Newbery was a bookseller, and an astute one at that. He was among the
first to appreciate the commercial possibilities of the children's book market,
and he also understood the methods needed to sell his wares. These consisted of an awareness of the moral climate of his time and an appreciation
of the value of self-advertisement. His works were always carefully titled,
so as to assure both parent and child of instruction *and* amusement. In his
stories, rewards for good behaviour usually managed to include an advertisement for others of his publications, or else somewhere in the book 'our
good friend in St Paul's Churchyard' would be mentioned. Although his
books always had a didactic purpose, on the whole the intentions were not so
obvious as to spoil the tale. Unlike the productions of the next century, the
information in them related much more to moral standards and polite
behaviour than to the acquisition of facts. At the same time Newbery
realized that some attempt at entertainment would make his work more
popular with the young, who in their turn would clamour for more publications by him. He was among the first to consider publishing specifically for
children and to issue books for home consumption rather than for school.
From then on publishers became fully aware of the need to provide reading
matter for children, though there was still little attempt to adapt it for
different age groups. Nor was it thought necessary to consider what children
might like, nor always to be concerned greatly about the way in which the
books were produced. Nevertheless the recipient of one of Newbery's
publications must have been quite delighted to receive a small squarish
volume, bound in Dutch gilt paper, and containing simple but vigorous
woodcuts. After all, these books were written and illustrated for *children*, and
this was in itself something of an innovation, and better by far than their
having to make do with works purloined from their parents' library.

A MAD TEA-PARTY.   103

'*Twinkle, twinkle, little bat!*
How I wonder what you're at!'

You know the song perhaps?"
    "I've heard something like it," said Alice.
    "It goes on, you know," the Hatter continued,
"in this way:—

'*Up above the world you fly,*
Like a teatray in the sky.
                    Twinkle, twinkle————'"

Here the Dormouse shook itself, and began

4 ALICE'S ADVENTURES IN
WONDERLAND by Lewis Carroll, with
. . . illustrations by John Tenniel.
Macmillan & Co, 1866. The
publication of *Alice* brought a new
element into children's reading. The
change is clearly shown here in the
parody of 'Twinkle, twinkle, little
star' by Jane Taylor. This poem was
first published in *Rhymes for the
Nursery* in 1806 and, like those of
Watts, had been learned by
generations of children.

Top:

5 A LITTLE PRETTY POCKET-BOOK,
INTENDED FOR THE INSTRUCTION AND
AMUSEMENT OF LITTLE MASTER TOMMY
AND PRETTY MISS POLLY. WITH TWO
LETTERS FROM JACK THE GIANT-
KILLER; AS ALSO A BALL AND A
PINCUSHION; THE USE OF WHICH WILL
INFALLIBLY MAKE TOMMY A GOOD BOY,
AND POLLY A GOOD GIRL. Worcester,
Massachusetts, Isaiah Thomas, 1787.
10 cm. First published by John
Newbery in London in 1744, this was
the first Worcester edition. Not only
does the title vary slightly from the
English version, but some minor
adjustments have been made in the
text.

Bottom:

6 THE HISTORY OF GOODY TWO SHOES,
OTHERWISE CALLED MARGERY TWO
SHOES, WITH HER MEANS OF ACQUIRING
WISDOM AND RICHES. Printed and sold
by Darton & Harvey, 1793.
11 × 8 cm. This very popular tale
was issued in various versions well
into the nineteenth century. A great
deal of instructional material was
included in this particular edition,
although some of it seems to have
been dragged into the story in a very
arbitrary way. In the same way the
dog in this illustration probably only
appears because a block was
available.

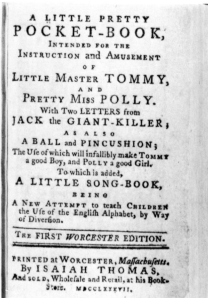

Instruction with Delight.

A LITTLE PRETTY
POCKET-BOOK,
INTENDED FOR THE
INSTRUCTION and AMUSEMENT
OF
LITTLE MASTER TOMMY,
AND
PRETTY MISS POLLY.
With Two LETTERS from
JACK the GIANT-KILLER;
AS ALSO
A BALL and PINCUSHION;
The Use of which will infallibly make TOMMY
a good Boy, and POLLY a good Girl.
To which is added,
A LITTLE SONG-BOOK,
BEING
A NEW ATTEMPT to teach CHILDREN
the Use of the English Alphabet, by Way
of Diversion.
THE FIRST *WORCESTER* EDITION.
PRINTED at WORCESTER, *Massachusetts.*
By ISAIAH THOMAS,
And SOLD, Wholesale and Retail, at his Book-
Store. MDCCLXXXVII.

In the second half of the eighteenth century, a number of people in Britain and America began to compose books they considered suitable for children, and which they hoped parents would also consider suitable. This did not prevent the continued publication of a certain amount of hack work. Publishers, realizing that children formed a new and somewhat undiscriminating market, were quick to take advantage of the fact. Having chosen a suitable title, and having available some spare woodcut blocks which might be sufficiently relevant for a juvenile book, a publisher would commission a story or series of tales to be woven around the illustrations. One of the results of this was that illustrations of different proportions might be used in the same story, while on other occasions it was clear that the pictures were by different hands. Sometimes the inclusion of a picture was obviously forced. A good example occurs in one of the editions of *Goody* 6 *Two-Shoes*, where the following passage is found:

Soon after this, a present was made to Mrs Margery, of a little dog Jumper, and a pretty dog he is. Pray look at him.

It is quite obvious that the dog had no particular part in the story, and had merely been introduced because the publisher had a suitable woodcut in stock. This practice could on occasions be seen in books for adults as well as for children; moreover the same illustration might re-appear in another book in a totally different context.

As the eighteenth century drew to its close, there appeared a number of writers for children whose works were destined to become staple fare in nurseries and schoolrooms well into the next century. Chief among these was Maria Edgeworth (1767–1849), whose writings were based on experiences within her own large family of brothers and sisters. Sarah Trimmer (1741–1810) also produced many works which were to have a long life among English-speaking children, and which were also frequently translated. Among them was *Fabulous Histories*, later known as *The History of the Robins*. This book, which was written to teach children the proper treatment of animals, also indicated a widening of the original narrow scope of religious and moral subjects. Indeed, throughout the later part of the eighteenth century, a new concept was at work, which derived from the publication in 1767 of Rousseau's *Émile*, with its softening influence on the harsher Puritan tradition of England and America. From Rousseau derived such ideas as the naturally good child corrupted by society, the supremacy of reason, and the concept of learning from experience, all of which found a place in continental juvenile literature. Bernardin de Saint-Pierre's *Paul et Virginie* (1787), which incorporated many of Rousseau's notions, was translated into a number of languages including English. In England these ideas were incorporated by Thomas Day in his *History of Sandford and Merton*, 1783–89, a work which Darton calls 'Rousseau for the English'. The same sentiments penetrated many other books of the time, as well as appearing in various translations from *L'Ami des Enfans* of the Abbé Berquin (1749–91). A selection from this work had a long vogue under the title of *The Looking-Glass for the Mind*, first published in 1787.

A number of books published for children at this period included a foreword addressed to the parents. It is from these prefaces that we can gather much information about the attitude to the child and his reading. Some offered merely straightforward advice, as in *The Polite Lady* of 1788, wherein a mother carefully explained to her daughter in a series of letters the sort of books she should read: 'good and sensible books . . . [are] a most rational employment and a most agreeable amusement'. They should consist in particular of history, than which nothing 'can afford more profitable instruction or more delightful entertainment'. With history went geography, and from the study of these two the daughter might 'acquire the knowledge of the world without the danger of being infected by its bad example'. The Abbé Fénélon had been tutor to the grandson of Louis XIV and his educational theories won wide respect. The English translation of Fénélon's *On the Education of Daughters* (published in France in 1687) made a number of points which were subsequently taken up by writers for children: 'Children should not be excited to talk; but as they are ignorant, and know but few things, they have consequently many questions to make. . . . The curiosity of children is an inclination of nature which takes the lead of instruction. Do not fail to profit by it. For example, in the country they see a mill, and they wish to know what it is. . . . Always show him [the child] the utility of what you teach him; make the usefulness appear with regard to your commerce with the world, and the duties of your station. . . .' This sort of approach, re-emphasized by ideals inspired by Rousseau, was taken up with enthusiasm by many of the late-eighteenth-century and early-nineteenth-century didactic writers. The 'question and answer' conversational framework was frequently used, often as no more than a mere skeleton for whatever information was to be conveyed. Everyday occurrences were utilized for instructional sessions, even as Fénélon had suggested. A good example of this was to be found in Maria Edgeworth's *Frank*, a work for quite young children, in which every walk or meal or aspect of daily life was used to provide some form of instruction on the part of the ever-attentive parents.

In view of the great influence exerted by Maria Edgeworth's books (which also appeared in translations), not only during her own long lifetime, but also on many of her younger contemporaries both English and foreign, it is interesting to read the opinions and advice offered to parents in her preface to *Early Lessons*, 1801. She pointed out how far things had progressed now that parents no longer attempted to cram children: 'they endeavour to cultivate the general powers of the infant understanding instead of labouring incessantly to make them reading, writing and calculating machines. . . . In the little books that follow [the volumes of *Early Lessons*] different parts of them are suited to the tastes of different children, as well as to children of different ages. . . . In choosing books for young people, the enlightened parent will endeavour to collect such as tend to give general knowledge and to strengthen the understanding. Books which teach particular sciences or distinct branches of learning should be sparingly employed. In one word, the mind should be prepared for instruction.' In this, Miss Edgeworth shows herself to be of the eighteenth century rather than the nineteenth; for by then almost every subject was considered suitable to be taught to the child, or at least explained to him, and no field of instruction could wait on the more general approach that she suggested; the world had appeared to grow too wide in the intervening years. She recommended to parents various books, including Mrs Barbauld's *Lessons for Children*, while from the Bible she particularly selected the narrative of Joseph and his brethren. 'When children can read fluently, the difficulty is not to supply them with entertaining books, but to prevent them from reading indiscriminately. To give them only such as cultivate the moral feeling and create a taste for knowledge, while they, at the same time, amuse and interest.' She then listed further suitable books, and commented on the early teaching of history. 'Entertaining story or natural dialogue, induces the pupil to read; but on the other hand, unless some useful instruction be mixed with this entertainment, nothing but mere amusement will be acceptable, and it will be difficult to bring the attention to fix itself, without dislike, upon any serious subject.' She then followed Fénélon in suggesting the usefulness of drawing instruction from everyday things, the method we know she herself employed in her own books – although she obligingly says, 'it is by no means intended to recommend that *lectures* should be spoken at every meal!' This sort of approach, she appreciated, was not possible for every parent, nor was every parent willing to spend so much time on the child, but of course she was writing for the middle and upper classes, at a time when servants were cheap, and the governess not always considered as even an upper servant. Maria Edgeworth's views were particularly interesting in that they were also reflected in other books for children produced in France, Germany and America at about the same time, and they indicated the evolution that was taking place in writing for the young as eighteenth-century ideas merged into nineteenth-century concepts.

In many European countries the early part of the nineteenth century was an era of transition, resulting from such factors as the War of American Independence in 1776, the outbreak of the French Revolution in 1789, the long drawn-out European wars which followed it, and the effects of the first stages of the Industrial Revolution. In England it was a period of industrial and social upheaval, as well as a continuation of the change in moral and religious standards,[1] which was to transform the regency rake into the serious-minded Victorian. The various effects of these changes will be dealt with in subsequent chapters of this book. One important result of technical developments taking place in different countries, as far as the present work is concerned, was an improvement in the quality of book production and illustration. A greater variety of instruction was now being provided for the young. But even as the educators were in full flow a certain amount of undermining had already commenced. In 1823–26 appeared the first translation of Grimm's fairy tales, originally published in Germany in 1812–18, and this, like *The Butterfly's Ball* of 1807, was symbolic of a new era which lay ahead, when children would be permitted to read for pure enjoyment; certainly, after the publication of *Holiday House* by Catherine Sinclair in 1839, Lear's *Book of Nonsense* in 1846, and still more so after *Alice* in 1866, juvenile reading could never be the same again.

In Britain the vogue of the 'toy book' commenced soon after the accession of Queen Victoria in 1837. Though these picture books made some attempt to include didactic material, it was rarely done with any very serious intent. Such books formed an important class of children's reading (and one which was peculiar to the English-speaking world), even if only because they were both numerous and varied. The majority of the 'toy books' were published simply to entertain, and their popularity between about 1850 and 1890 was

7 GERMAN POPULAR STORIES. Translated from the *Kinder und Haus Märchen* collected by M. M. Grimm, from oral tradition. C. Baldwyn, 1823. 17 × 10 cm. This first edition of what was to become known as *Grimm's Fairy Tales* was illustrated by George Cruikshank. Its appearance marked the first real relief from the religious, moral and didactic barrage to which the young were subjected. Edgar Taylor's translation of these tales was no doubt popularized by the choice of such a well-known artist to illustrate the text, and the title-page shown here indicates the spirit in which Cruikshank approached his task.

[1] *Before Victoria: changing standards and behaviour, 1787–1837*, by M. Jaeger, 1967.

17

indicative of a changed emphasis in juvenile leisure reading. The prosperity of the British Victorian middle class was accompanied by the idea of 'self help', a concept which encouraged and expected the intelligent worker to try to rise into a higher station in life. The new mobility brought about by the railways led everywhere to a change in society's traditional values while new patterns of education emerged, in some instances following the work in England of Thomas Arnold at Rugby School. As the nineteenth century progressed the Education Acts passed in various countries permitted learning to filter further down the social scale, eventually resulting in somewhat less rigid class divisions. This survey really ends before the close of the nineteenth century since by then technical progress in methods of illustration and book production, and social change brought about by compulsory primary education in many countries, had together begun a radical transformation of reading matter for both adults and children.

Many of the types of book to be considered in this survey are still read today – the alphabet book, the easy reading book for beginners, the Biblical tales, the animal story and so on. But just as we are aware now that these books are by no means the whole extent of children's reading, so it is important to bear in mind in the chapters that follow that large areas of children's literature have been merely touched on. My concern here has for the most part been with didactic material, and for more than a century now this has formed only a portion of the vast output of writing for the young.

1 On the Illustration of Children's Books

Before considering techniques of illustration or even the illustrations in children's books themselves, it is as well to pause a moment over the whole subject of pictures in books. These days we are so bombarded with pictorial matter that much of it passes unnoticed. It is much more difficult for us than it would have been even for our grandparents to imagine a world with few public pictures. By public I mean those pictorial representations of one sort or another which surround us in street, shop or home. The nearest we can get is to imagine ourselves in a small village, where there are no hoardings or posters, the village shop has no goods on display in the window and passing vans do not advertise their wares in pictorial form on their sides. But even now, once inside the village shop, we shall probably find packages covered with pictures, while display boxes likewise proclaim their contents. At home in our mythical village, apart from illustrated news-papers and journals, we shall probably have the service of a travelling library offering many books with pictures. Should we not wish to read, then most of us have access to that idol of the eyes, television.

In view of this surfeit of visual material it is hard to place ourselves in the position, say, of our eighteenth-century forbears. There was at that time no absence of actual *colour* in life, such as we now take for granted in the printed matter around us, but there was a *comparative* absence of representational popular art. There was no advertisement art such as we know today, nor were goods contained in gay alluring packaging; books and journals were also far less wide-spread, even among the literate population.

It is against this background that we shall consider the illustrations provided in contemporary juvenile books. When pictures were rare, each one had far greater impact than we can appreciate now. There are few children who reach school age today without having some idea of what is meant by the word 'elephant'. Judging by some of the illustrations we shall see in this book, people in the past – even the illustrators themselves – could live all their lives with only a hazy idea of this strange animal. And if the importance of illustration in conveying the exact form of physical objects should be doubted, let this animal be described *in words only* to three people who have never seen an elephant, and there will be three differently drawn interpretations of it. With the visual over-familiarity which we enjoy concerning the world around us, we have lost much of the wonder that was expressed in earlier books. Sitting at home, we can see in the greatest detail all the wonders of Rome, we can explore remote regions of the con-tinents, and the moon and the stars are brought within our sitting rooms. But the excitement of the pre-pictorial traveller has largely gone. When we get to the Colosseum it looks just like the photographs, of which we have probably seen many. How different from the early traveller, who, right up to the middle of the nineteenth century, had to be content with an artist's drawing, made on the spot and subsequently engraved by someone who himself had probably never been there. In a manuscript diary of 1816

on which I have been recently working, the writer complained that, having
bought a print of a view of Pisa to familiarize himself with the town before
he arrived, he was indignant to find when he got there that it was physically
impossible to see the scene as the artist had depicted it!

Many books were not illustrated at all. Not only were pictures rarer, but
before the middle of the nineteenth century few books were printed in
colour; those that had any colour in them would have it put in by hand,
probably by the method of child labour. Most illustrators worked
anonymously; it was almost the middle of the nineteenth century before it
became common for artists to be acknowledged as frequently on the title-
pages of children's books as they were on those for adults.

When we think about modern children's books, it is the artist's name that
is recalled as often as the author's – sometimes of course they are one and
the same. We talk about 'a Sendak book' or 'a Wildsmith book', unaware
of any incongruity in referring to a book by its illustrator rather than by
the writer of its text.

The illustrated book has a long history; if we include illuminated manuscripts we can trace it back to the early Middle Ages or even before that. But
although certain illustrators gained a reputation over that long period,
many remained unknown, or their work was recognized only by a name or
set of initials placed in the corner of a print. So it is not surprising that
illustrators of children's books also received small credit, especially when
writing for children was itself less regarded. Even so, all pictures had to
originate with someone. Sometimes they were merely re-drawings or re-
cuts of existing originals in an adult book. If an outstanding artist did work
for children's books, he did not always care to lend his name to the title-
page. However, the later work of Thomas Bewick in the last years of the
eighteenth century made such an impact on book illustration in general,
that his was one of the first names which began to appear with any frequency
on title-pages of children's books; 'cuts after Bewick' may only have been a
way of selling more copies, but it was significant of changes to come.

An example of the change of emphasis can be seen in the work of someone
not obviously connected with children's books at all. Sir Henry Cole was a
friend of the Prince Consort and a man who had a finger in many pies baked
in the mid-nineteenth century, including the Great Exhibition of 1851 in
London. He was appalled at the standard of children's books when he came
to buy books for his own children. As a direct result of this he published,
from 1841 onwards, a series of books known as *Felix Summerly's Treasury of
Pleasure Books for Children* (Felix Summerly was one of Cole's pseudonyms).
Apart from the content of these books, which is not our concern at the
moment, the illustrations were commissioned from some of the best-known
artists of the day, and their names were often acknowledged. Cole was
greatly concerned about the illustration of books for children, and was
probably the first to write about the subject seriously. In the Library of the
Victoria and Albert Museum, London (of which Cole was the first

Director), there exists his own copy of *Traditional Nursery Songs of England*. He had stated his disapproval of the idea 'that the lowest kind of art is good enough to give first impressions to a child', and so for this work he had commissioned several artists who had exhibited at the Royal Academy, including J. C. Horsley and C. A. Cope. In his personal copy of the work, there are two sets of the illustrations; one was produced by lithography and was by far the better of the two; the second was produced by wood engraving, in which the finer line of the first set has been largely lost. More interesting still are Cole's own comments on the illustrations and the method of their production, which he has written in the book itself:

> One object of the Home Treasury series . . . was to place good pictures before my own and other children – Cope, Horsley, R. Redgrave, Webster, Mulready, all Royal Academicians, with Linnell, Townsend and other artists, made designs in lithographic ink which were coloured by hand. This process was costly and each tale had to be published at 4s 6d in 1840 – whilst in forty years afterwards works by Walter Crane with excellent designs are sold at about one tenth the price. After the first edition of the Nursery Songs an edition was produced by means of coloured woodblocks, with inferior results.

Other artists of note beside Bewick had also illustrated books for children. Among these was George Cruikshank, whose work had embellished the first English translation of Grimm's fairy tales in 1823–26, and who went on to write and illustrate his own version of four popular fairy stories in the 1850s. Nevertheless, like Edward Lear in 1846, or Charles Henry Bennett during the same period, these were the exceptions; early children's book artists usually preserved their anonymity, some with only too much cause. But the great period of the 1860s when the quality of English book illustration reached a peak also influenced children's books, and just as the adult books appeared with lists of artists and engravers in them, so did the better class of children's books. By this date Walter Crane had already produced the first of his toy books (1866), and Tenniel had created the Wonderland creatures as we know them today. The children's book artist need no longer be an anonymous worker and could, if he wished, confine himself almost entirely to the juvenile market. Nevertheless, the hack illustrator has continued to be employed at all times in certain types of children's literature, and this is still so today.

We will now consider the various technical processes of illustration available to the publisher during the eighteenth and nineteenth centuries. By the time printing from movable types had become acclimatized in Europe, many people were already familiar with woodcut illustration. Single prints made from wood blocks had circulated in the fifteenth century, but such illustration was perhaps more familiar in the form of illustrations to cycles of events, of which the *Biblia Pauperum* was the best known example. Before the spread of printing, pictures would have been widely

9 TRADITIONAL NURSERY SONGS OF ENGLAND. With pictures by eminent modern artists. Edited by Felix Summerly, 2ed., with additions. Joseph Cundall, 1846. 16 × 12 cm. 'Felix Summerly' (Sir Henry Cole) helped to make nursery rhymes respectable by publications such as this. The book from which this illustration comes was his own copy, and contains both the woodcut and lithographed version of the pictures, together with his own comments on them.

accessible only in the form of stained glass or mural painting – neither of which was obviously either portable or personal. The woodcut enabled many copies to be produced from the same block and was the first step towards popularization of pictures. Moreover it was a process particularly suited for combination with printing, since in each case an impression on a sheet of paper was produced from a raised surface. For centuries to come, the cheapest method of illustrating books was by the woodcut or wood-engraved method. Low costs of production were particularly important to the publisher considering children's books, especially in the eighteenth century when the importance of the children's market was as yet un-appreciated, and when the meanest of illustration was often considered quite good enough for such books. Nearly all early children's books were illustrated by this method – when they were illustrated at all. The woodcut or wood engraving need not be either cheap-looking or nasty; in the hands of a Bewick or the English illustrators of the 1860s it could become an object of great beauty, and its potential has also been appreciated by artists today. At its best, it has a magical, evocative quality that leads the mind on and into the picture. At its worst, it could be an unintelligible smear on the page, crudely cut and badly printed. Far too many of the eighteenth- and early nineteenth-century children's books showed the woodcut illustration at its poorest. Frequently a tiny picture, encircled by a frame of black lines, portrayed a figure, whose features appeared to have been shaved away by a slip of the knife or graver, standing stiffly in a room. That it *was* a room, was indicated by a roughly sketched chair, table or window; a tree could suggest an outdoor scene.

Another method which could be used for book illustration was the engraved plate. This had also been used at the close of the Middle Ages and, like the woodcut, could exist independently of books. Traced with a graver or burin on copper plate (later, steel was more commonly used), engraving was an intaglio process; i.e. the ink which was to make the impression on the paper, was forced into a line incised into the surface of the plate. Since printing was a raised process and engraving (together with its sister process of etching) was an intaglio process, the two could not be produced simultaneously, as was possible with the woodcut. Inevitably its use put up costs. Engraved illustrations were usually printed on pages separated from the text, sometimes facing it, sometimes facing one another. Occasionally engraved illustrations might be placed in spaces left for them in the text itself, but this was much more common in the more expensive adult book. Although more costly in the initial outlay, engravings had an advantage over woodcuts in that the plates did not warp or crack, though in the course of much use the sharpness of line could deteriorate. It was the linear quality that made engraving particularly attractive in certain kinds of children's books, especially those where detail or line was important – maps are an obvious example, but other subjects such as natural history could also benefit. It was a process especially popular in the first few decades of the nineteenth century, and was frequently used in the publications of John Harris of London, one of the great purveyors of educational books for the young at that period; it was also used in similar American works of the same period. Following the new techniques inspired by Thomas Bewick and his pupils in the early part of the nineteenth century, however, there was a great improvement in wood engraving, until in its brilliance and treatment of detail it would rival the intaglio process.

The third process which might be used for book illustration was lithography. A late-comer to the field, it was invented by a German, Alois Senefelder (1771–1834), at the end of the eighteenth century. Like the intaglio processes, it was expensive, since it could not be used in conjunction with letterpress, being a planeographic process. It was based on the antipathy of oil and water. A picture was drawn on limestone with a grease-based chalk; the stone was then soaked with water and a roller with printer's ink passed over it. The ink would only adhere where the chalk had marked the stone, and when a sheet of paper was placed under heavy pressure upon the surface, the original design would print off. Although not greatly used by itself in children's books at the beginning, it was the development and subsequent application of this technique which was to have the most important effect on the illustration of children's books in the later part of the nineteenth century, and indeed on modern book illustration. The use of lithography was rather more common on the continent than in Britain or America in children's, as in adults' books; but such pictures, though often of a higher quality, were of necessity far fewer in number owing to the higher cost of the lithographic process.

So far we have only considered black and white illustration. Illustration in colour is a comparatively new development and all the early children's books were illustrated in black and white only. Where colour was added, it was put in by hand, and this applied to adult books too. In the first half of the nineteenth century it was not uncommon to issue children's books in two forms: plain and coloured. The colouring was frequently put in by child labour, sometimes under a 'factory system', or occasionally as work at home. At its best, hand-coloured illustration had great delicacy of tint and subtlety of tone, and it gave great charm to the page it decorated. But far too often it deteriorated into great washes of colour splashed in somewhat random fashion over the subject. Since for economy's sake it was necessary to complete as many examples as possible, the colouring of the individual illustrations would be divided up among the workers: one doing all the faces, another the coats, another the trees, and so on, each with one colour to add to the whole. In this book, wherever the term 'hand-coloured' is used, it means that the work concerned was issued with the pictures already coloured; where they have been subsequently coloured by the child owner, this is always clearly stated.

The nineteenth century was a period of great technical development, and the search for a good colour process was one of many problems that received attention during the first few decades of the century. Colour printing had to be good, cheap, and suitable for book illustration. The first break-through in this field in Britain was made by George Baxter of London in the 1840s, but although the result was effective, it was not cheap to produce and the Baxter process never became a really viable proposition. The lead passed to Baxter's former apprentices who developed a method of colour printing based largely on his work and pursued under licence. Children's books now began to glow with colour, not all of it very subtle. After the bright, clear tints of the water-colours to which children had been accustomed, the crude vigour of chromo-lithography must have seemed startling, and the idea that children's books should be brightly coloured still prevails today. Towards the end of the century, however, in the work of a printer like Edmund Evans, the colours became toned down, and in the illustrations of Randolph Caldecott and Kate Greenaway there was a reversion to the lighter colouring of the earlier period.

After the development of chromo-lithography and the coloured woodcut, the next important stage in the technique of illustration was the advent of photography. Not only did artists themselves take advantage of this new medium but it could also be used in the actual production of the printed picture. Since the use of photography and the photographic processes in children's book illustration occurs at the end of the nineteenth century it is of less importance in this book than the other methods discussed. The progress from black-and-white photography to the almost ubiquitous use of colour in books is something which many of us have seen take place in our own lifetime. It is now nearly always possible to illustrate any given subject exactly according to its shape and colour, so that children today are far better informed from a visual point of view than their predecessors when every picture had to be hand-drawn, hand-engraved and then probably hand-coloured. Nevertheless, in spite of the exactness now possible, there is still a need for the type of illustration that stimulates the imagination and creates atmosphere. When this is so the artist frequently reverts to the old techniques of wood engraving or lithography, even if the published result in today's books is achieved by mechanical means rather than the hand techniques of former times.

The above is only a brief introduction to the subject of techniques of book illustration and takes no account of the mechanical developments which took place during the period under consideration. This aspect can be studied elsewhere.[1] Here it is only important to say that it indicates the background of different methods of reproduction and changing techniques against which we shall consider actual examples of children's book illustration, especially those used to sugar the pill of instruction in books for the home.

10 A BOOK OF NONSENSE by Edward Lear. Frederick Warne & Co [*c.* 1870?]. 26 × 23 cm. First published in black and white in 1846, Lear's *Book of Nonsense* was an important landmark in juvenile literature. A book without any didactic aim, it helped bring about a slow change in the attitude to children's reading.

[1] *Victorian book design and colour printing*, by R. MacLean, 2ed, 1972.

A
BOOK of NONSENSE.

BY EDWARD LEAR.

There was an Old Derry down Derry, who loved to see little folks merry;
So he made them a Book, and with laughter they shook
At the fun of that Derry down Derry.

LONDON:
FREDERICK WARNE AND CO.,

BEDFORD STREET, COVENT GARDEN.

NEW YORK: SCRIBNER, WELFORD, AND CO.

2 Alphabet Books

Alphabet books are basically of two kinds: those that set out to teach the alphabet as a preliminary to reading, and those that use the ABC merely as a frame within which to portray any chosen subject. Simple alphabet books were rarely illustrated in the early period; all that was needed was to show the shapes of the letters. It was soon realized that the young mind would recollect more easily if learning were made more palatable and so the letters of the alphabet began to be associated with rhymes of mnemonic form. Some of these were to prove ephemeral; others, such as 'Great A, little A, bouncing B' and 'A was an archer and shot at a frog', were to have a long life from the eighteenth century onward. It was this expanded form of the alphabet which no doubt encouraged the earliest form of illustration. The idea of personalized or illustrated letters, however, was not new; in medieval manuscripts initial letters had frequently sprouted figures and faces, a tradition which had been continued on occasions by woodcut initials. Moreover, many a sixteenth- and seventeenth-century copybook had offered an alphabet made up of human figures so disposed as to represent the various letters, a genre that was to have a long life.

Early alphabet books had a purely didactic aim. They consisted for the most part of the letters of the alphabet in various forms: both capital and small letters, in roman and italic, and often in 'black letter' (or gothic) as well. In some cases the letters would be followed by the syllabary and a few simple words or phrases; it was the latter which eventually attracted illustration. However, quite early in the eighteenth century there appeared books which showed a letter together with a woodcut picture – but without words; occasionally not even letters were shown but only pictures arranged in alphabetical order of the objects depicted. Exactly how this helped a child to learn its alphabet is hard to see but, like most of the ABC books, it certainly presupposed an ever-present governess or parent.

These crude pictures, with or without letters, were among the earliest pictorial alphabet books, and the same picture blocks might be recognized

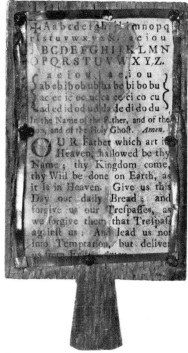

Opposite:
11 THE ALPHABET OF OLD FRIENDS. G. Routledge & Sons [1874]. 27 × 23 cm. An illustration from a book by Walter Crane, one of the leading book artists of the day. Its object was to give pleasure to a child, rather than to teach the alphabet.
Above:
12 HORNBOOK. Late eighteenth or early nineteenth century. 11 × 6 cm. Many hornbook frames were made of leather; this one, however, is of unvarnished wood. On it has been pasted down a printed alphabet, syllabary and the Lord's Prayer.
Left:
13 THE SILVER PENNY FOR THE AMUSEMENT AND INSTRUCTION OF GOOD CHILDREN. York, J. Kendrew [c. 1820]. 9 × 6 cm. In this example, both forms of the initial letter are shown close to the word to which they relate, but the rhyming text is scarcely suitable for the young learner and the woodcuts could appear equally well in other contexts.

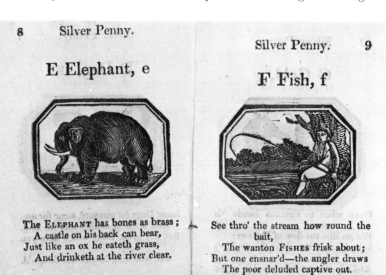

8   Silver Penny.

Silver Penny.   9

E Elephant, e

F Fish, f

The ELEPHANT has bones as brass;
    A castle on his back can bear,
Just like an ox he eateth grass,
    And drinketh at the river clear.

See thro' the stream how round the bait,
    The wanton FISHES frisk about;
But one ensnar'd—the angler draws
    The poor deluded captive out.

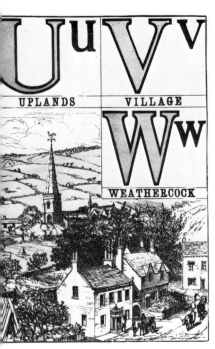

14 THE FARMYARD ALPHABET.
G. Routledge & Sons [*c.* 1870?].
25 × 19 cm. A colour-printed 'toy
book', to which modern parallels
could be found. The detail and
competence of the illustration shown
here indicates the increasingly
sophisticated approach to children's
books.

again, re-appearing in simple readers. A rhyming alphabet readily lent
itself to illustration, but even here there was little concern for relevance.
The picture of a dunce, horse or dog might be used to illustrate the letter
with which the word began, but equally it might be made to fit a rhyming
couplet. The crudity of the verses matched the quality of the hack illustrations, and emphasized the comparative unconcern for the standard of
children's books which characterized this early period. The alphabet was
the key to all the child's subsequent learning, and was a hurdle to be
surmounted as soon as possible with the minimum of fuss; certainly
eighteenth-century books indicated little desire to linger over such a
basic chore.

By far the most interesting and attractive types of alphabet books came
later. On the whole they presupposed a knowledge of reading beyond the
beginner stage. Some of these *may* have helped a struggling learner, but most
of them used the alphabetic scheme only to describe or picture a particular
theme. There was a spate of these in the Victorian period, and towards the
end of the nineteenth century they were taken up by artists such as Walter
Crane, who raised them to a very high artistic level. The later works
frequently continued to use the old style of descriptive rhyming couplets to
ensure effective remembrance in young minds and, together with improved
colour illustrations, they may well have achieved their aim. Alphabet
books of all kinds are still produced today and, since there is a revival of
interest in teaching very young children to read, both the 'basic recognition'
style ABC's and the 'framework' kind are published.

As with all the early children's books, the alphabet books are perhaps
equally interesting for the picture they give of the contemporary scene.
They had little literary merit since most of the verses which accompanied
the illustrations continued (as indeed some still continue) to use the jog-
trot rhythm of 'A was an archer and shot at a frog, B was a butcher who had
a fine dog' (though it must be admitted that this type of verse is very suitable
for infant learning). The very nature of the alphabet book precluded any
sustained text so that, apart from the sociological aspect, their only interest
today lies in the pictorial quality and in the method of presentation.
Within the genre there was a surprising amount of variety – the placing of
the material on the page, the competence or otherwise of the drawing and
colouring, and the memorability, of lack of it, of the text. Unlike some of
the later children's learning books, the alphabet books concerned themselves almost exclusively with the familiar world of the child; or, if they
extended that world, it was still to something within the child's compass.
Perhaps in such a work as *The Alphabet of Flowers*, 1852, there was a desire to
instruct the young learner in the names of the flowers, but even then they
tended to be flowers with which the child would be familiar. And so the
day-to-day world of the child is brought before us, and with it a way of life
now unfamiliar to many, from such simple examples as *The Farmyard* 1
Alphabet (*c.* 1870) with its picture of a vanishing rural life, to the *Railway*

Is the FOG, that in winter we find
Often causes the train to be hours behind.

Is the GUARD, that sits perched up above,
And sees that no parcels or passengers move.

Is the famous HOTEL of the town,
Where gentlemen stop when by rail they come
down.

15 RAILWAY ALPHABET. T. Dean & Son [1852]. 24 × 17 cm. One of several books which were issued with this title during the second half of the nineteenth century. This example has hand-coloured woodcuts.

15 *Alphabet* (*c.* 1852), with its portrayal of the then exciting new method of transport. Even the earliest alphabet books emphasized the familiar, but today's reader is constantly brought up against the thought that while the child *might* have learned his alphabet this way, surely he could never have been able to read the words that went with the letters. Presumably he would have memorized the text or words in parrot fashion, even as many children do today. Anyone who has read a story a number of times to a small child will know how any deviation is immediately noticed. Reading of the words and rhymes must have come later, but no doubt as the child struggled to recall the order of letters (an item of knowledge we grown-ups take so much for granted) the helpful rhyming couplets must have come gratefully to his mind.

12 Obviously the instruments of a child's earliest instruction should be as indestructible as possible. The hornbook admirably fulfilled this require-ment and had an honourable lineage. There is an early portrayal of one in an illustration to *Margarita Philosophica* by Gregorius Reisch, published in 1503: a child who is being encouraged to commence the acquisition of

knowledge is seen clasping a hornbook in his hand. Hornbooks were so
called not because they were made of horn but because a piece of transparent horn was used as a protective agent, in the way that a piece of
perspex might be used today. Nor were they books, but rather single sheets
of paper (or occasionally vellum) mounted on a piece of wood or leather and

roughly about 11 × 16 cm in size. Printed or written on the paper would be the alphabet, sometimes showing both capital and small letters and roman and italic type. Other items fitted into the remaining space might include the Lord's Prayer, or the syllabary, or numbers from one to ten, or perhaps a few basic words. The text was covered with a sheet of transparent horn and provided with a handle, rather similar to those on the guides occasionally to be found in churches which the visitor carries round in his hand. The hornbook could be fastened to the child's girdle and could be used (in view of its fairly solid nature) in play – it has always been particularly associated with the game of shuttlecock. This was the basic type of hornbook but there were others. Grander households might have hornbooks of silver or ivory, while for general school use they might be made of brass.

A development of the hornbook was the battledore (or battledoor) and both were widely used in England and America. In spite of the name, battledores can never have been used for the game, since they were made of cardboard. They usually consisted of much the same items as the hornbooks, either printed or engraved. The text was pasted on to one side of a piece of

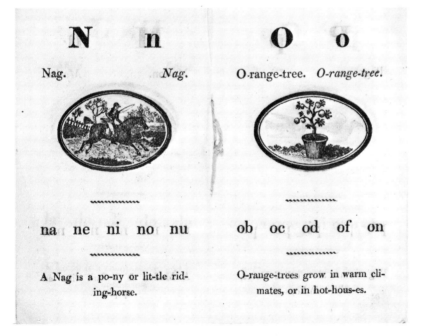

18 THE CHILD'S INSTRUCTOR; OR, PICTURE ALPHABET. Glasgow, Lumsden & Son [c. 1820]. 10 × 6 cm. A chapbook with hack illustrations, presumably meant for a child beyond the alphabet stage, since the texts are scarcely suitable for the youngest learner. The syllables shown under the woodcut illustration have little relation to the sentence which follows, and must have seemed very confusing to a child.

cardboard, while the other side was frequently adorned with woodcuts. The cardboard was then folded in two, or perhaps as in plate 17, into three. The fact that the battledore offered twice as much space as the hornbook encouraged some publishers to add illustrations, or even rhymes. The battledore first appeared about the end of the eighteenth century, but

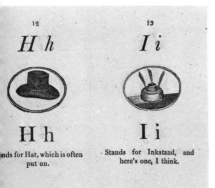

H h   *I i*

H h   I i

...nds for Hat, which is often   Stands for Inkstand, and
put on.   here's one, I think.

Above right:
19 AN ALPHABET AND READING BOOK.
Late eighteenth century? 10 × 9 cm.
One of many crudely illustrated
alphabet and reading books, which
shows a complete lack of appreciation
of the child's learning needs. Not
only are the pictures difficult to
recognize, but the mixture of
upper and lower-case letters would
be very confusing for a beginner.
And who is to blame him if he says,
'N for horse' or 'Y for sheep'!

Above:
20 THE SILVER TOY; OR, PICTURE
ALPHABET FOR THE ENTERTAINMENT
AND INSTRUCTION OF CHILDREN IN THE
NURSERY. Wellington, F. Houlston &
Son [before 1828]. 10 × 6 cm. A clear
and simple chapbook alphabet, of a
kind that might be found today.

examples are to be found as late as the middle of the nineteenth century;
stylistically they changed little, and the dating of examples is always
difficult unless adequate clues are present.

Simultaneously with the hornbook and the battledore there appeared
other works designed to teach the alphabet. But for the most part the early
instruction which appeared in book form did not concentrate on the
alphabet only; on the contrary, the ABC was treated rather summarily. The
eighteenth-century alphabet book usually included the syllabary, some
spelling examples, and a certain amount of reading matter (which was not
always as easy as might be expected from a 'first' book). An early example
of this rather crude type of alphabet book is to be seen in plate 18. It is
always difficult in such early examples to make the distinction between an
alphabet book which included some simple reading, and a reading book
which also included the alphabet as a preliminary. In plate 19 is shown an
opening from a typical late eighteenth-century or very early nineteenth-
century book of this type. Unillustrated pages with the alphabet precede
this illustrated opening, which shows crude cuts printed on coarse paper,
with lettering which is almost unreadable. Would the contemporary child
have been able to recognize the pictures, even with the aid of initial letters?
It is very doubtful. Nevertheless, this type of illustration continued to be
considered good enough for children's books for some time to come. The
same style of illustration is to be found in the many chapbook versions of
the alphabet books, the printing of which flourished in a number of centres
in Britain and America, especially in the first decades of the nineteenth
century. 'Chapbooks' were the hand-sized publications carried round the
country by the 'chapman' or pedlar, and included reading for the unsophisticated as well as for the young. As well as London, towns such as
York, Coventry, Derby, Wellington, Edinburgh, Glasgow and Banbury
were among the many active publishing centres for chapbooks in England,
while in America they were printed mainly in Boston, New York,
Philadelphia and Worcester. Three examples, from Edinburgh, Glasgow
and Wellington, are illustrated here, all produced between 1815 and 1830 at
the latest, and a slightly earlier one from New Haven (USA). They show the
different styles which were current in this type of book. Each offered a

20 simple framed cut, but only in *The Silver Toy* do the illustrations appear at
18 all relevant. In *The Child's Instructor* and *The Silver Penny* (a title also used for
22 publications from Philadelphia and New Haven) the picture could equally
well have applied in a completely different context. Moreover, in the one
book in which the illustration looked as though it had been specifically
chosen for the text, *The Silver Toy*, so little care was taken with the layout that
the matching rhyme to each picture appeared on the *next* page rather
than on the opposite one. However, even in the chapbook type of alphabet
book an effort was occasionally made to meet the child's needs. In *A New*
21 *Lottery Book*, 1819, not only were the cuts relevant, the rhymes apt and the
layout appropriate, but an ingenious attempt was made to relate the
pictures directly to the child's learning:

THE LOTTERY DIRECTIONS

As soon as the child can speak, let him stick a pin through the side of the
leaf where the pictures are, at the letter on the other side, which you
would teach him; and this let him do, till he has by many trials run
the pin through the letter, turning the leaf every time he sticks the pin
through, by which means the mind of the child will be fixed so long
upon the letter, that he will have a perfect idea of it, and not be liable
to mistake it for another.

Then shew him the picture opposite the letter, and make him read
the name of it; which you will find divided, if it be a word of two or
more syllables.

When he has learnt the Roman letters, you must teach him the
Italic ones in the same manner, and then the figures.

At the same time as the small chapbook versions of the alphabet were
circulating, a move had already begun towards the type of book to be
known later as the 'toy book'. This was usually about 25 × 17 cm in size,

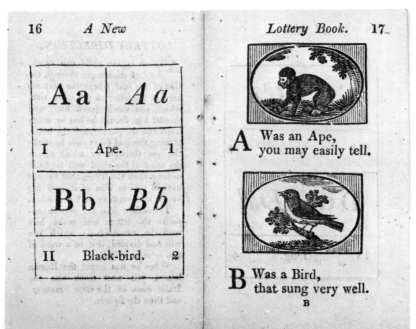

Left:
21 A NEW LOTTERY BOOK ON A PLAN
ENTIRELY NEW DESIGNED TO ALLURE
LITTLE ONES INTO A KNOWLEDGE OF
THEIR LETTERS &c BY WAY OF
DIVERSION. Edinburgh, Caw & Elder,
1819. 10 × 6 cm. In this chapbook, a
real attempt has been made to meet
the needs of the young learner. The
illustration shows how the page-
spread makes a complete unit, with
the various versions of letters and
figures on one side, and clear
woodcuts with simple rhyming
couplets on the other. The book also
included an ingenious method of
teaching the alphabet by means of
a pin.

Above:
22 THE SILVER PENNY; OR, NEW
LOTTERY-BOOK FOR CHILDREN by
J. Horner. New Haven, Sidney's
Press, 1805. 10.5 cm. A work with a
similar title was published in the
same format in England about 1820
(see plate 13).

I is an Infant, and dressed out in silk.

J is a Jug, to hold water or milk.

frequently printed on one side of the page only, and containing about eight
leaves. Within this general description there was every kind of variation.
Some books had text on the inside covers only; others had it below the
illustrations; yet others alternated the textual and illustrative material.
Moreover, the genre was extremely long-lived. Becoming popular in the
1840s, it was taken up in Britain with gusto by Crane and Caldecott in the
1870s and 1880s. The 'toy book' was most suited to using the framework of
the alphabet as an excuse to depict almost any subject. Many of them were
not strictly books from which to learn the alphabet, though perhaps read
aloud and embellished with attractive and relevant pictures, such books
may have helped in this basic chore. A good example of the type is to be seen
in plate 23, where the child would be encouraged to memorize the rhyme, 2
note the letter, and work out for himself the other items beginning with the
same initial. Similar to this is plate 24; each letter is surrounded by a series 2
of items beginning with the same initial letter, though here again it is
doubtful whether the child at the alphabet stage could manage to read
words like 'knocker'. *New Stories About the Alphabet c.* 1850 went a stage 3
further in producing simple reading texts to emphasize the letters of the
alphabet (as well as providing interesting social information for the modern
reader). But the continued use of hack illustrations is still visible in the way
that the illustration of 'wagon' has obviously been taken from another
source.

The simplified 'letter + word' has had a long life and continues down to
the present day – only the style and the competence change. The advent
of good colour printing permitted the production of books like *The Farmyard* 14
Alphabet which could still be appreciated by the modern child. But it is with
such mid-century productions as the *Railway Alphabet* and *The Alphabet of* 1
Nations that we see how the letters of the alphabet have become merely an
excuse for picture or rhyme: and very attractive they are, these hand-
coloured productions of the 1850s. But Kate Greenaway's version of *A*
Apple Pie, produced in 1886, is very sophisticated indeed, and reaches a 2
style which, even in its own day, must have attracted the adult as a work of
art in a way that the earlier, cruder children's books can never have done.
In the *Alphabet of Old Friends* by Walter Crane, published in 1874, we have 1
left all attempt to teach far behind – the 'old friends' were the nursery ryhme
characters who appeared in this composite picture, and whose identifica-

S SANG FOR IT

THE FLY.

What a nice Fly here is, Mamma!

Do not keep it in your hand, my dear;
let it go.

Go, Fly! Mamma says I must let you go.

Good child; a Fly is so weak, you cannot hold it in your hand without hurting it.

Die La=ter=ne.
Das Lamm.
Der Leuch=ter.
Der Löf=fel.
Die Licht=schee=re.
Der Lö=we.
Die Lei=ter.
Der Luft=bal=lon.
Der Luft=schif=fer.
Die Lam=pe.
Die Lan=ze.

Man braucht die La=ter=ne, um Licht zu be=hal=ten,
wo sol=ches im Frei=en durch Wind und Luft=zug leicht
aus=lö=schen könn=te. Mit dem Löf=fel ißt man die
Sup=pe. Die Lan=ze ist ei=ne ge=fähr=li=che Waf=fe.
Der Lö=we ist eins der stärk=sten Raub=thie=re. Man
nennt ihn den Kö=nig der Thie=re.

U u is the first letter in Urn.

Our Urn is set upon the table, at tea-time, full of hot water for mamma to make the tea with. Tea is the leaf of a plant that grows in a distant country, and the leaves, when gathered, are dried, to make them ready for use.

V v is the first letter in Vessel.

All ships are called Vessels, yet some are named brigs, sloops, barks, &c. Perhaps this one is going to China, to fetch tea; or to the West Indies, for sugar and coffee. I hope she will have a good voyage, and return safe.

W w begins Wagon, The Wagon is made wide and long, to carry a great many goods. See what fine horses there are to draw it. The man who drives a Wagon is called a Wagoner; he is very proud of his horses, and calls each of them by its name.

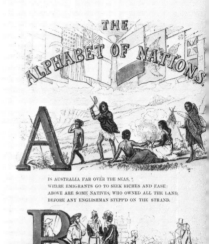

tion was contained on the printed page (not reproduced) opposite the illustration. Here is a picture, an artistic entity in itself, by one of the great book artists of the day, in which there is no hint of anything save a desire to give pleasure in its perusal.

The examples of alphabet books discussed in this chapter are but a few taken from the enormous number published over a period of two hundred years, both for pleasure and for learning, for the very young and for the not so young. All except the hornbook and the battledore can be found today, and even, sadly enough, the crudely illustrated hack work is still with us. In spite of all alternative methods of teaching, by blocks or puzzles or other devices, the alphabet book will no doubt continue to be the child's first book, as it has been through the centuries.

Opposite left:
29 ONE, TWO, BUCKLE MY SHOE. G. Routledge & Sons [1873]. 25 × 18 cm. The illustrations to this traditional counting rhyme are treated throughout with the sophistication that Walter Crane brought to all his work on children's books.

Above left:
30 NEW STORIES ABOUT THE ALPHABET. Dean & Co. [*c.* 1850]. (Grandmama Easy's series). 25 × 17 cm. This alphabet book certainly required an attendant governess, nurse or parent – but it was never too early, it was thought, to start this sort of instruction for the young.

Above:
31 THE ALPHABET OF NATIONS. W. Tegg & Co. [1857]. 27 × 21 cm. In this type of alphabet book the letters form a frame within which to display a sequence of rhymes and pictures on a particular subject.

3 Reading Books

The alphabet was the key to reading, and reading was the key to the Bible and to salvation. This was the idea that lay behind much early instruction in reading, especially among the Protestant populations of Europe and America. This close link between reading and the Bible was not confined to the eighteenth-century instigators of the Sunday-school movement; it was shared by all who had the welfare of children at heart. Those who advocated Sunday schools intended to bring the benefit of religion to the poor, but it was not meant that as a result of their ability to read and write they should attempt to rise to higher things. Nevertheless increasing industrialization demanded higher standards of literacy. In Britain for example, the Reform Acts of 1832, 1867 and 1884 required progressively more and more education, as the vote was allowed to larger sections of the population. The same was equally true of course in other European countries, and also in the New World. But it was to be literacy taught in a formal way, usually in scholastic institutions; because we are dealing here with the early reading books used in the home, we are almost exclusively concerned with middle and upper-class material. In passing, it might be mentioned that even now, when primary education is universal, the *subject matter* of reading books is still only rarely adapted to the background of the working class child.

Reading itself progresses naturally from the alphabet, and reading books do likewise. It is often difficult to decide whether a work was an alphabet book with some reading material or a reading book which included the alphabet among its preliminary matter. Since reading was a means of making personal contact with the Word of God, it was many years before it was thought suitable that the printed word should be used to provide a means of entertainment. Children especially were considered to be in need of rescue from their naturally wicked propensities, and so their earliest reading material was intended to provide religious and moral instruction, while at the same time teaching the actual ability to read. The fact that hornbooks and battledores often included The Lord's Prayer did not mean that the child could read the words, since he had probably learnt them parrot fashion; but it did indicate the importance placed on the reading of religious texts, starting from the child's earliest years. Early reading books for children seem to demand a high standard of the infant learner, though of course it was expected that an adult should be present when such instructional books were being used. Up to about the middle of the eighteenth century there seems to have been little appreciation of the limits of childish capacity, or of the differences between one age group and another. But as the century progressed, we detect greater awareness of this limitation, indicated by efforts to compose books with examples using from two to four letters, or one to four syllables, according to the child's age. Nevertheless in spite of this grading, the child was expected to progress quite quickly to more complicated works. By the middle of the eighteenth century there had appeared a further attempt in many countries to facilitate learning to read by the use of the 'split-word' system, in which

32 THE NEW-ENGLAND PRIMER IMPROVED. FOR THE MORE EASY ATTAINING THE TRUE READING OF ENGLISH. TO WHICH IS ADDED, THE ASSEMBLY OF DIVINES, AND MR COTTON'S CATECHISM. Boston, S. Kneeland, 1762. 10 × 8 cm. A very popular early American book for children, which went into many editions. The same couplets, also illustrated with cuts, are to be found in some contemporary English primers; a version of them appears in *A Guide for the Child and Youth*, published in Glasgow in 1750.

long words were broken up into their component syllables, for the benefit of the very young reader. The effect on pronunciation of this method of helping children to master the intricacies of reading must have been quite extraordinary since each syllable tended to get the same emphasis; nevertheless the system remained in use until the present century.

Reading being one of the earliest accomplishments, it was particularly suited to be taught at home. Many eighteenth and nineteenth century reading books put their texts in the form of dialogues between mother and child, thus giving a naturalistic background to the child's learning. Fortunately they supply us with an invaluable insight into the everyday life and speech of the contemporary child. From these readers we learn of his meals ('butter is not good for little boys'), his hours of work and play, of a comfortable background of maidservants and nurses, of rewards and treats and punishments, and we are also reminded of the darkness that lay in wait outside the comfortable sitting room or nursery, with its array of bright candles.

Having mastered the alphabet, the child would then be expected to familiarize himself with the syllabary. This system of putting together the vowels and consonants must have seemed a very arbitrary piece of learning, especially as the groups of syllables were often unconnected with any other matter included on the same page. This hurdle surmounted, the child could then turn to 'real' reading. What did he find? The cheaper books for children were not always very attractive: printed on coarse greyish paper, with indifferent small type, some of the reading matter must have proved hard going for the little learner. Where illustrations were provided, they sometimes bore so little relation to the text that they offered no help. On the whole few really simple reading books were published until towards the end of the eighteenth century, and of course there was no reason for them to be illustrated at all. Unlike all the other subjects to be considered in this work, reading books were free to range over any and every topic, but on the whole they endeavoured to keep close to the child's everyday experience. Nevertheless, since it was intended that every book should be didactic, we find moral and religious tales included among the earliest reading matter for

33 LEÇONS POUR LES ENFANS DE TROIS À HUIT ANS. (Lessons for Children from Three to Eight Years Old) par Mistriss Barbauld. Première partie. 2ed. Paris, 1817. 11 × 9 cm. These two illustrations show the frontispiece (above) and title-page (opposite) of Mrs Barbauld's *Lessons for Children*, a work which had a long vogue in England. The frontispiece is a hand-coloured engraving.

the very young. One such beginners' book was *Reading Made Perfectly Easy; or, an Introduction to the Reading the Holy Bible; Consisting of Lessons so Disposed, that the Learner is Led on with Pleasure from Easy to More Hard Words. . . . Being Sentences from Scripture and Other Books on Moral and Religious Subjects. . . . Very Pleasant and Advantageous to Youth* [etc]', by T. Dyke (29th edition, 1785). The author noted in his preface, 'I have also added proper cuts to the histories, to allure little ones to take delight in reading'. But the book cannot have offered much to delight the young reader, being cramped to look at and full of difficult words. Moreover, in common with much infant reading, it had nothing to encourage the child to read on, to make him want to know what happened next, which is the surest way to stimulate reading.

There were, however, some writers for children who showed an appreciation of what was needful in a first reader. One of these was Mrs Barbauld, whose works were long popular in both Europe and America. Her *Lessons for Children from Two to Three Years Old*, first published in 1778 in London and in 1788 in Philadelphia, was particularly admired in Britain and America, and was also translated into French. Mrs Barbauld also provided sequels to bring it up to the level of older children. In her preface she explained her method for attracting the young child: 'A grave remark, or a connected story, however simple, is above his capacity; and *nonsense* is always below it; for folly is worse than ignorance. Another great defect is the want of *good paper a clear and large type*, and *large spaces*'. Although the physical requirements of books for the young were stated thus early, it was rare that any publisher took heed of them, and even later editions of Mrs Barbauld's own books fell short of what she deemed necessary. Nevertheless, she showed an understanding of childish capacity which few others had done, and her books were nearly always illustrated. Here are some examples from the opening section of *Lessons for Children*:

Come hither, Charles, come to mamma.
Make haste.
Sit in mamma's lap.
Now read your book.
Where is the pin to point with?
Here is a pin.
Do not tear the book.
Only bad boys tear books.
Charles shall have a pretty new lesson.
Spell that word. Good boy.
Come and give mamma three kisses.
One, two, three.
Little boys must come when mamma calls them.
Blow your nose.
Here is a handkerchief.
Come and let me comb your hair.

Stand still.
Here is the comb case for you to hold.
Your frock is untied.
Stand upon the carpet.
Do not meddle with the ink-horn.
See, you have inked your frock.
Here is a slate for you, and here is a pencil.
Now sit down on the carpet and write.
What is this red stick?

This was the simple everyday world of the child, with words which he would know from daily conversation. But there was nothing to stimulate the imagination, nothing beyond the factual and the commonplace. Although the children for whom this book was written would surely be too young to read for themselves, there was little to make it attractive to the adult for reading aloud, nor anything to make the child wish to learn more of the text. The passage quoted above came at the beginning of the book, and though the work became progressively more difficult, the general tenor remained low.

There was (and is) a big jump for a child to make when he goes from reading aloud to 'silent reading', and in earlier centuries this jump must have been less necessary. The mention of reading aloud is a reminder that much more of this took place in previous centuries than is at all common now. Since amusements were largely home made, and travelling abroad in search of entertainment was often restricted by weather and various local conditions, for the more comfortably off there were long evenings – and even days – to be filled. Reading aloud was one of the common family pastimes. The women could settle to their sewing while readings from the latest novel or their favourite poet took place. We may recall the disappointment of the younger members of the Bennet family in *Pride and Prejudice*, when Mr Collins, invited to read aloud, chose to entertain them with a book of sermons. Also in favour of communal reading were the living conditions of the time. Heating was confined to the main parts of the house, and a move away from the communal room often meant a plunge into instant darkness, unless one carried with one a frail candle, which was liable to be extinguished in the all-too-frequent draughts. There was every encouragement to sit together in common warmth and light, and since concentrated individual occupations would be difficult in such circumstances, reading aloud was popular. This was as true of the nursery as the drawing room. No doubt the young child, always eager to emulate his elders, would strive for proficiency in order to take his turn in the nursery or family readings. This sharing of reading among different age groups, even within the nursery society, may account for the advanced nature of some of the 'first' readers (could the *ABC du Premier Âge really* be for the very young?) since the writer could for the most part count on a learner being

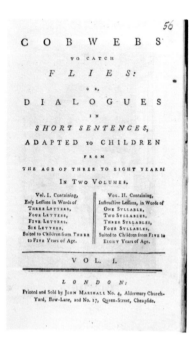

C O B W E B S

TO CATCH

F L I E S:
OR,

D I A L O G U E S
IN

SHORT SENTENCES,

ADAPTED TO CHILDREN

FROM

THE AGE OF THREE TO EIGHT YEARS

IN TWO VOLUMES.

| Vol. I. Containing, Easy Lessons in Words of Three Letters, Four Letters, Five Letters, Six Letters, Suited to Children from Three to Five Years of Age. | Vol. II. Containing, Instructive Lessons, in Words of One Syllable, Two Syllables, Three Syllables, Four Syllables, Suited to Children from Five to Eight Years of Age. |

V O L.   I.

L O N D O N:

Printed and Sold by John Marshall No. 4, Aldermary Church-Yard, Bow-Lane, and No. 17, Queen-Street, Cheapside.

Above:

34 COBWEBS TO CATCH FLIES; OR, DIALOGUES IN SHORT SENTENCES, ADAPTED TO CHILDREN FROM THE AGE OF THREE TO EIGHT YEARS [by Lady Fenn]. J. Marshall [1783]. 16 × 10 cm. Published anonymously by Lady Fenn, this work not only proved popular in its own day, but was frequently imitated. The title-page of the first edition is shown here.

Right:

35 COBWEBS TO CATCH FLIES; OR, DIALOGUES IN SHORT SENTENCES, ADAPTED TO CHILDREN FROM THE AGE OF THREE TO EIGHT YEARS [by Lady Fenn]. J. Marshall [1783]. 16 × 10 cm. Taken from Volume I of the first edition, this double-page spread shows the spaciousness of the layout and the relevance of the illustrations. 'The Toilet' is a good example of how everyday occurrences and phrases were included in the text, and of the social insight they provide for the modern reader.

surrounded, in those days of full nurseries, by a whole group of brothers and sisters.

That this was so is suggested by the 'Address to all good children' which prefaced the work whose title has been borrowed by the present book, *Cobwebs to Catch Flies; or, Dialogues in Short Sentences, Adapted to Children from the Age of Three to Eight Years.* This was first published anonymously in 1783; its author was Lady Fenn, who, under various pseudonyms, was responsible for a number of didactic works in the last quarter of the eighteenth century. Her 'Address' reads:

You all love to see something which is new; so I do not doubt but you are eager to see your new books. I speak to you as good children; so I conclude that the eldest looks at my books first; to the eldest then I speak: You can read any words which you meet with; therefore I shall not confine myself to short words, but give you the pleasure of obliging your brothers and sisters, by reading my address aloud to them, after which you will resign my first volume, to one of the younger children, who is only able to read words of three letters; and he will be amused with my dialogue about the Cat, whilst he gratifies the curiosity of the little happy circle, and enjoys the satisfaction of entertaining the whole family.

Cobwebs to Catch Flies was also interesting in that it broke away from the tiny format of many of the earlier reading books for the young. There was

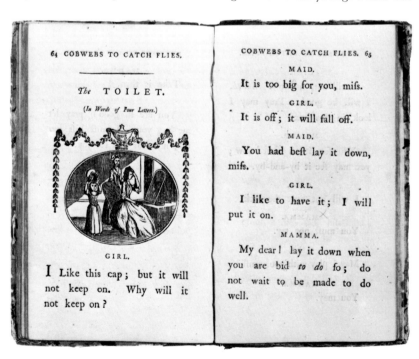

64 COBWEBS TO CATCH FLIES.

The T O I L E T.

(*In Words of Four Letters.*)

GIRL.

I Like this cap; but it will not keep on. Why will it not keep on?

COBWEBS TO CATCH FLIES. 65

MAID.

It is too big for you, miss.

GIRL.

It is off; it will fall off.

MAID.

You had best lay it down, miss.

GIRL.

I like to have it; I will put it on.

MAMMA.

My dear! lay it down when you are bid *to do* so; do not wait to be made to do well.

an air of spaciousness about the pages and this was aided by the large type; the illustrations, though simple, related clearly to the text to which they referred. In its 'short sentences' the book used the progressive method mentioned earlier, starting with three- to six-letter words in volume I, and with one- to four-syllable words in volume II. The dialogue form used in *Cobwebs* made the work into a series of small playlets, and in this it differed from many of the nineteenth-century books, which used dialogue more as a series of sparsely interrupted monologues.

There was very little change in the type of reader used in the nineteenth century; indeed many of the eighteenth-century works continued to be printed throughout most of the next century. Not all of them were quite so attractive as *Cobwebs to Catch Flies*, and many of them took a much more serious approach to the matter of learning to read, for by the early years of the nineteenth century there were many more subjects to be absorbed. One work, which its author published 'from a conviction that much good will be derived by its being used as a first reading book for little children', was *Green's Useful Knowledge, for Little Children. Bein* [sic] *a Looking Glass in which They may See the Dangers of Childhood Without Feeling their Effects*. Published about 1845 this book was written in simple language and made use of the 'split-word' technique, and it was well illustrated with woodcuts. But it was full of the most gruesome episodes about children who were disobedient, inquisitive or careless, and who ended by getting burnt, drowned or mutilated – all without the writer expressing one word of pity for their fate. This may have been an extreme case, and no doubt many parents preferred a less terrifying approach. Nevertheless, we may recall that Alice, confronted by a bottle that said, 'Drink me', remembered that ' she had read several nice stories about children who had got burnt, and eaten up by wild beasts, and other unpleasant things, all because they *would* not remember the simple rules their friends had taught them: such as,

37 ALPHABET ILLUSTRÉ; 100 vignettes et lettres ornées (Illustrated Alphabet; 100 vignettes and decorative letters). Tours, 1867. 16 × 10 cm. This combined alphabet and reading book is of a kind that could also be found in England or America during the same period. It shows, too, the universality of the 'split word' method of teaching.

that a red-hot poker will burn you if you hold it too long; and that, if you cut your finger *very* deeply with a knife it usually bleeds. . . .' But one thing was quite certain, that from his earliest attempts at reading the child would be thoroughly indoctrinated along the religious, moral and behavioural way his parents wanted.

Although so many of the early readers must have appeared formidable to the beginner, it was obvious that the writers attempted to make them attractive. The titles of these books were very revealing; they did try to encourage the learner: *The Infant's Friend: or, Easy Reading Lessons for Young Children*, 1824; *Youth's Best Friend; or, Reading no Longer a Task*, 1829; *The Royal Primer: or, Easy and Pleasant Guide to the Art of Reading*, c. 1800; *Aunt Mary's New Year's Gift to Good Little Boys and Girls who are Learning to Read*, 1819. 'Easy' and 'pleasant' were two favourite words, but it sometimes seems as if the authors had long forgotten their own struggles with words. A book like *Youth's Best Friend; or, Reading no Longer a Task*, certainly showed full appreciation of the help provided by plenty of illustrations. But when we consider it more fully, the arbitrariness of the pictures on the left-hand page did not greatly assist the child struggling with the accompanying text, a long list of 'words of two syllables'. The right-hand page, with its (for us) very charming toyshop picture, lacked any link with the lesson on the opposite page, while some of the sentences below presumed a considerable ability in the young reader.

These problems were not confined to the English-speaking child, though English is a notoriously difficult language to learn to pronounce. Looking through some of these early reading and spelling books, English-speakers may be glad that they are long past the struggle with 'cough' and 'bough' and all the other traps for the unwary reader. We have already noted that Mrs Barbauld's *Lessons For Children* was translated into French, so that similarities between works in different countries is not surprising. *Alphabet* 3

then did cry so much that the nurse thought she was hurt ; but when she told her what the mouse had done, she said she was glad of it ; and that it was a bad thing to wish to eat it all, and not to give a bit to John.

Lesson 4.

Miss Rose was a good child, she did at all times what she was bid. She got all her tasks by heart, and did her work quite well. One day she had learnt a long task in her book, and done some nice work ; so her Aunt said, you

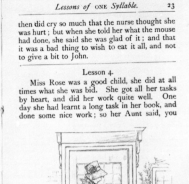

Lesson 3.

I knew a nice girl, but she was not good : she was cross, and told fibs. One day she went out to take a walk in the fields, and tore her frock in a bush ; and when she came home, she said she had not done it, but that the dog had done it with his paw. Was that good ?—No.

Her Aunt gave her a cake ; and she thought if John saw it, he would want to have a bit ; and she did not choose he should ; so she put it in a box and hid it, that he might not see it. The next day she went to eat some of her cake, but it was gone ; there was a hole in the box, and a mouse had crept in, and eat it all. She

Top:

A combined spelling and reading book, first published in 1801, which had a long popularity. In this edition the illustrations are by Kate Greenaway, one of the foremost children's book illustrators of the day, who was prepared to place her talent at the service of a didactic work of this kind.

Bottom:

A book illustrated by Harrison Weir, the well-known animal artist whose work often appeared in books for the young. The simple text 'in words of one syllable' consists of a series of short stories which encouraged the child to read further – a change from the stilted passages of many early reading books.

Illustré, 1867, despite its title, was more of a reader than an alphabet book – given English words it could have been equally at home in Anglo-Saxon nurseries. Here were to be found the same style of illustration and even the same method of 'split-word' reading. Likewise the *ABC und Lese-Buch*, 1846, showed that a common method of approach was being followed in German reading books too. That this latter work was popular is proved by the fact that the volume illustrated here had quickly gone into a third edition.

Probably few English language books were of such apparently recurring popularity as William Mavor's *English Spelling Book*, first published in 1801. As late as 1885 a new edition was produced, with illustrations by

Kate Greenaway, then one of the foremost children's book artists. The general appearance of this book, with its reasonably spacious layout and attractive pictures, showed how far children's books had progressed since the beginning of the century. Nevertheless, its text still looked back to the older style of reading matter. More significant for the future was *The Man's Boot, and Other Tales; or, Fabulous Truths in Words of One Syllable*, 1876. For 3 here, following the well-established method of keeping to words of one syllable for the benefit of the youngest reader, a book had been published which told a series of connected tales in such a way that a young reader would want to know what happened next, and this is surely the best incentive to reading. Moreover, the illustrations were by Harrison Weir, whose name appeared on the title-page in large letters, while the author of the text concealed his identity. Weir was a fine illustrator whose name was associated with many animal books, for both adults and children. Here, therefore, we have a well illustrated and well produced reading book, with simple stories that could hold the childish interest and stimulate imagination. Other writers also developed this idea so that even such 'undidactic' tales as those of 'Reynard the Fox' were written in monosyllables for the benefit of very young readers.

When he had at last mastered the art of reading, a whole world of knowledge, in book form, lay before the juvenile reader. What use was made of his reading ability we shall see later on. Fortunately for the child, the works we shall consider here were only half the story, for, with the arrival on the scene of *Alice* in 1866, imagination had finally overcome didacticism, and reading had become the key to a magic door.

4 Counting Books

Counting books, rather like books on grammar or music, do not readily lend themselves to illustration. A simple exercise with counters is worth all the counting rhymes. Nevertheless, attempts were made with this subject, as with other (apparently) equally unpromising ones, to present it in memorable pictorial form. The majority of these efforts were not very successful; no doubt they merely added to the confusion in the child's mind. But even if they did not greatly assist the children for whom they were intended, they frequently provide an interesting insight into the economic background of the period for the modern reader.

Learning to count is one of the child's earliest lessons, coming close to the alphabet in priority. For this reason counting rhymes have a long history, and many have the status of nursery rhymes: 'One, two, buckle my shoe' is an example of this kind. Counting books can come in various forms. They may simply attempt to teach the child his numbers; they may go further and offer the multiplication table or simple sums; or they may even explain the complexities of the currency. The recitation of numbers has a rhythmic quality, and this makes them particularly suited for expression in verse form – and it was quickly appreciated that children find verse more memorable than prose.

It is among the books dealing with numbers that we find one of the most charming of early books for children, and one of the most successful of its kind. This was *Marmaduke Multiply's Merry Method of Making Minor Mathematicians*, published by John Harris in 1817. What child could resist the alliterative charm of its title – or what adult either? Its rhyming couplets were perhaps less memorable than its title, and some of them limped very badly. But, with their pretty accompanying hand-coloured illustrations, they must have assisted many a child in his task of learning the multiplication tables.

Seven times 10 *are* 70.
We're sailing very pleasantly.

Seven times 11 *are* 77.
I always make my bread with leaven.

By XII, my morning's work is done;
And I am free till half-past I;
And so I play till I o'Clock,
At marbles, top, and shuttlecock,
At half-past I, I hear the chime,
Which tells me it is dinner-time.

en from 28 take 14,
hen 14 still remain,
carpenters so often seen
shave the wood with
plane.

btract 15 from 21,
nd 6 will then appear,
printers, printing one by
one,
oks quite correct and clear.

om 25 next take 18,
nd 7 will then be found,
bakers, who nice bread
do bake,
ith flour that's finely
ground.

Above:
42 AMUSING SUBTRACTION. Dean & Son [*c.* 1850]. (Cousin Honeycomb series). 25 × 17 cm. Whether this 'toy book' really helped the young learner may be doubted but, unlike the *Addition* (plate 45), at least it uses the same subject (printers, bakers) throughout each verse. The original illustrations are hand-coloured.

Right:
43 JACKO'S MERRY METHOD OF LEARNING THE PENCE TABLE. Dean & Co. [*c.* 1850]. (Grandpapa Easy's series). 25 × 17 cm. This 'toy book', whose title is probably a deliberate echo of *Marmaduke Multiply*, attempts to relate the pence table to the objects illustrated. A charming if somewhat arbitrary result is achieved. The original cuts were hand-coloured.

Less successful in its own field is *Prittle Prattle's Clock, c.* 1845. At first 41 sight, the layout of this book, with its simple pictures and large, clear print, seems ideal for the young learner; its rhymes too, have an attractive rhythmic quality. But on the pages shown, there is no illustration of a clock face, although the book purports to assist in learning to tell the time, and the text must have been very confusing for any child trying to distinguish his figures. A number of counting books were published in 'toy book' form in the middle of the nineteenth century; we find *Amusing Subtraction, Amusing* 42 *Addition* and so on. But most of these books failed to appreciate an essential factor in teaching numbers to a young child, namely that the 'count' must

fifty? "Only that the mile-stone near our house has fifty miles marked on it," said Fanny.   That will do, said the short man.

> Friends now oft greet each other's smiles,
>   By railroad's speedy aid;
> And fifty pence clear fifty miles,
>   Or four and two-pence paid.

I see that smiling little fellow in the middle has something to say for our next number, sixty: let us hear it.   "I have counted the buttons on your waistcoat," said William, "and there are just sixty."   Your counting is correct, said the man proudly; and Jacko looked as though he thought so too.

> My buttons placed in triple row,
>   The garment's price will tell;
> A penny each,—and sixty show
>   Five shillings, very well,

I see I've a customer for the next number; the young gentleman next

5

5 mal 10 ist 50.

Fünf mal zehn ist fünfzig —
Die Mädchen stricken Strümpf' sich,
Sie helfen früh der Mutter schon,
Und ernten froh ihr Lob als Lohn.

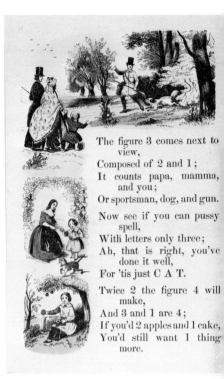

The figure 3 comes next to
    view,
Composed of 2 and 1;
It counts papa, mamma,
    and you;
Or sportsman, dog, and gun.

Now see if you can pussy
    spell,
With letters only three;
Ah, that is right, you've
    done it well,
For 'tis just C A T.

Twice 2 the figure 4 will
    make,
And 3 and 1 are 4;
If you'd 2 apples and 1 cake,
You'd still want 1 thing
    more.

refer to identical objects: a point which the Nicholas Bohny work fully appreciated. Using assorted items as part of the 'count' must have proved very confusing indeed. Nor would the rather muddled layout of the pages have helped comprehension. More successful perhaps was *Jacko's Merry Method of Learning the Pence Table*; the illustrations are firmly confined to the tops of the pages, and do not wander all over them to the detriment of the printed verses, as in the examples quoted above. Moreover, there was in *Jacko* an attempt to link currency and numbers to something more obvious, but it remains a rather tortuous way of making the pence table 'amusing'.

Das Ganze Einmaleins [1872?] was an attractive hand-coloured book of pictures, but its rhymes are no better than its Anglo-Saxon counterparts. Moreover here, too, the text is not closely related to the learning of numbers, and the illustrations must have appeared quite arbitrary to the young learner. But arbitrariness was not necessarily a deterrent, as the long life of 'One, two, buckle my shoe' proves. The text of this nursery rhyme is quite as unexpected in its sequence as any to be found elsewhere, and yet it has a lasting quality. Walter Crane's illustrations to the old favourite are clear and apt. For the contemporary child it must have been a treasure, with its wealth of detail and bright colours. In its time *Marmaduke Multiply* was no doubt equally attractive to his rather more colour-starved predecessor. Both stand out from the rest of their kind as examples of a successful marriage between text and illustration.

Above left:
44 DAS GANZE EINMALEINS IN LUSTIGEN REIMEN UND BILDERN (The Whole 'Twice-Times Table' in Jolly Rhymes and Pictures). Stuttgart, K. Thienemann's Verlag [1872?]. 20 × 16 cm. A German equivalent of the rhyming multiplication table book, with illustrations which are only marginally relevant. The example shows that weak rhyming verses were not confined to the Anglo-Saxon countries.[1] The illustrations are hand-coloured.

Above:
45 AMUSING ADDITION. Dean & Co. [c. 1850]. (Grandpapa Easy's series). 25 × 17 cm. A failure to appreciate the appropriate method to follow in teaching numbers is clearly shown in this example. What was a small child to make of spelling 'pussy' in three letters? The last verse mixes so many different ideas that childish logic would only be confused.

[1] Five times ten is fifty
The girls are knitting themselves stockings
They start to help their Mother early on
And happily earn her praise as pay.

5 Religious Instruction

Jesus promet à S. Pierre les clefs du ciel.

S. MATTH. JESUS étant venu aux environs de Césarée de
Chap. XVI. Philippe, interrogea ses disciples, & leur dit : « Que
v. 13-20. » disent les hommes touchant le Fils de l'homme?
S. MARC. » qui disent-ils que je suis? » Ils lui répondirent :
Chap. VIII. » Les uns disent que vous êtes Jean-Baptiste ; les au-
v. 27-30. » tres Elie ; les autres Jérémie ou quelqu'un des Pro-
S. LUC. » phètes. » Jesus leur dit : « Et vous autres, qui dites-
Chapit. IX. » vous que je suis? » Simon Pierre lui dit : « Vous êtes
v. 18-21. » le Christ, le Fils du Dieu vivant. » Jesus lui répon-
AN DE J.C. dit : « Vous êtes bienheureux, Simon fils de Jean :
32. » parce que ce n'est point la chair ni le sang qui vous
» ont révélé ceci ; mais, mon Pere qui est dans le ciel.
» Et moi je vous dit que vous êtes Pierre, & sur cette
» pierre je bâtirai mon Eglise, & les portes de l'enfer
» ne prévaudront point contre elle. Je vous donnerai
» les clefs du royaume du ciel : tout ce que vous lierez
» sur la terre, sera lié dans le ciel ; & tout ce que vous
» délierez sur la terre, sera délié dans le ciel. »

46 HISTOIRE DE L'ANCIEN ET DU
NOUVEAU TESTAMENT . . . AVEC UN
DISCOURS ABRÉGÉ AU BAS DE CHAQUE
FIGURE, QUI EXPLIQUE LE SUJET:
OUVRAGE UTILE POUR L'INSTRUCTION
DE LA JEUNESSE (History of the Old
and New Testament . . . with a Short
Discourse below each Picture to
Explain the Subject of it: a Useful
Work for the Instruction of the
Young). Paris, J. T. Herissant, 1771.
20 × 13 cm. A well illustrated work,
with most of the cuts by Nicholas le
Sueur, including the example shown
here. This type of book, which
combined the relevant texts from all
the Gospels, had been in use for
centuries.

One of the most important reasons for learning to read, particularly in Anglo-Saxon Protestant countries, was that the literate child or adult should be able to make direct contact with the Word of God, as contained in the Bible. The salvation of the soul was to many a primary consideration, but the means of achieving this differed. In the Catholic church there was greater emphasis on the interpretive mission of the clergy and the importance of the Mass. The extreme Protestant, on the other hand, considered that no one should come between him and the revealed Word of God. It was inevitable that the Puritan tradition in both England and America should place considerable emphasis on the reading of the Bible by each individual, and that as a result of this the seventeenth century in particular should see the rise of various religious sects, each with their own interpretation of certain Biblical phrases. In spite of various movements within the Catholic church, it never fragmented in the same way.

The importance of leading a good and godly life encouraged an early start to religious instruction for children, since a child was never too young to die, and thus to go to perdition unreclaimed. Born in sin, the child was considered to be inherently wicked until the light of the Gospel had been poured upon him and he had become conscious of his own sinfulness. This attitude coloured much of the reading provided for children over many years. First the child must read and learn the Bible stories, then he must appreciate the application of them and the Christian religion in his daily life. The consciousness of sin was strong among Puritans on both sides of the Atlantic, and since they were particularly literate, with each man aware that he had a knowledge of God's Word, it was among these people that some of the earliest religious writings specifically for children were to be found. Too much of the early writing, by people like James Janeway (1636?–74), was based on fear – fear of what would happen to the wicked. Children were exhorted by warnings and by pious examples to prepare themselves for death and judgement. And if we feel that this was rather unnecessary for the small child, we have to remember the high incidence of infant mortality, which made death far more familiar to the child of the past than it would be to his modern counterpart.

There were two ways of bringing religious knowledge to the child. One was by the direct method of making him read the Bible. But it was early realized that this was rather indigestible fare for the young, so versions and abridgements were published in Catholic and Protestant countries alike. Another much-favoured method was to provide books illustrating and elaborating religious truths, either in verse or prose. In both, the importance of pictures was not overlooked. Certain Bible stories had provided the subjects for the earliest illustration to be found in the West. Pictures of incidents from the Old and New Testament were to be found in nearly every medieval church, glowing with colour on walls or in windows.

Isaac Watts's *Divine Songs Attempted in Easy Language for the Use of Children,* 71
published in 1715, heralded a change in the type of religious instruction,

though not to the exclusion of the older, sterner, style.[1] Watts appreciated the need to allure children to learning by bringing every subject within their comprehension, which too many of the earlier writers had failed to do adequately. In his *Songs* he used simple rhyming verses, for he realized that this made for easier learning, and their background was the familiar, everyday world of the child. Such ideas, so new at the time, were yet so apt that generations of children, even into the twentieth century, took much of their early religious instruction from the charming, simple *Songs*. The scope of Watts's work can be deduced from the titles he gave his poems: some examples are 'Praise to God for our Redemption', 'The Advantage of Early Religion', 'Against Pride in Clothes', 'Love Between Brothers and Sisters' and 'Against Scoffing and Calling Names'. Watts's poems lent themselves readily to illustration and were to be found published in many forms, from crude chapbooks to the elegantly illustrated versions of the 1860s. Their popularity naturally attracted imitators, only some of whom had the same gift for understanding the child's mind that Watts possessed. The poems of Ann and Jane Taylor, members of the highly literate 'Taylors of Ongar' family, also had the same simple appealing quality of Watts's work, and *Original Poems for Infant Minds*, published anonymously in 1804, carried on the gentle tradition of the earlier writer.

7   The Bible was also offered in verse, and one of these, *The History of the Holy Jesus*, was especially popular in America. A metrical version of *The History of Joseph and his Brethren* was equally popular in both England and

---

[1] *Divine Songs attempted in easy language for the use of children*: Facsimile reproductions. . . . With an introduction . . . by J. H. P. Pafford, 1971.

Commandments of the Church.

TO HEAR MASS ON SUNDAYS AND HOLIDAYS OF OBLIGATION.

ND *the faithful* were persevering in the doctrine of the Apostles, and in the communication of the breaking of bread and in prayers.—*Acts* ii. 42.

Left:
47 THE HISTORY OF THE HOLY JESUS. . . . BEING A PLEASANT AND PROFITABLE COMPANION FOR CHILDREN; COMPOS'D ON PURPOSE FOR THEIR USE. BY A LOVER OF THEIR PRECIOUS SOULS. 6ed. Boston, J. Bushell and J. Green, 1749. 10 × 7 cm. One of the most popular religious books for children in America; it went into many editions. The text is in verse.

Above:
48 A PICTORIAL CATECHISM, AFTER ORIGINAL DESIGNS BY G. R. ELSTER. Engraved by R. Brend'amour. Under the direction of the Rev. M. B. Couissinier. Paris, A. W. Schulgen; London, John Philp (1861). 18 × 12 cm. An illustrated religious work aimed specifically at Roman Catholic children. It placed rather more emphasis on the teaching of the Church than most comparable Protestant works for the young.

The Introduction.

THE great eternal God, who made
    The World and all therein,
Made Man also upright and just,
    And wholly free from Sin.

A pleasant Paradise the Lord
    Prepar'd with beauteous Trees,
And all the Fruits thereof to Man,
    To eat whene'er he pleas'd;

But one, and only one, and sure
    That could not be tho' much,
But so it was, on Pain of Death,
    That Tree they might not touch.

For in the Day he eat thereof,
    God said that he should die,
And yet when Satan tempted him
    He eat immediately.

Adam and *Eve.*

And

America, as were the miniature 'thumb' Bibles by John Taylor, the Water-Poet. If versification made Biblical texts easier to memorize, illustration certainly helped to fix incidents in the child's mind. In addition to these metrical and illustrated editions of the Bible, another popular variant was *A Curious Hieroglyphick Bible*, published in London and in Worcester, Massachusetts. In this type of presentation certain words were replaced by hieroglyphics. For the benefit of the less competent, the interpretation of the picture was placed at the foot of the page. This was just as well, since it was obviously a struggle at times to illustrate the required word, and it became even more of a struggle to interpret it correctly. The effectiveness of this type of Biblical instruction may be doubted, since not only was the answer to the puzzle given on the page itself, but the method required so much space that only small (and usually unconnected) passages could be given. Nevertheless, its pictorial quality must have endeared it to many children, especially since it was the kind of reading which could be permitted on Sunday.

Books which could be read on Sundays were of considerable importance in the life of the late eighteenth- and early nineteenth-century child, largely

owing to the growth of the Sabbatarian movement. As Muriel Jaeger has pointed out in her book *Before Victoria*,[1] there was a considerable change in the moral and religious climate in England towards the end of the

[1] *Before Victoria: changing standards and behaviour, 1787–1837*, by M. Jaeger, 1967.

VINCENT BROOKS LONDON

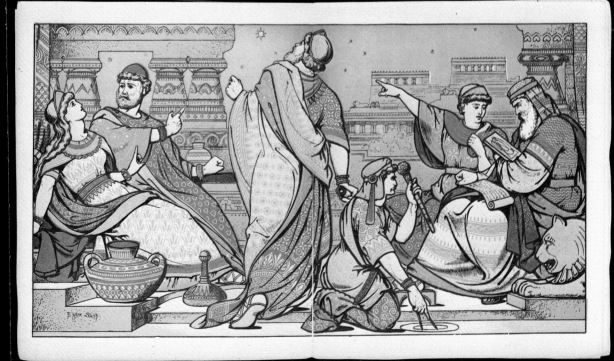

JOSEPH SOLD BY HIS BRETHREN.

WILLIAM DICKES, CHR

eighteenth century, a change which can also be traced in other countries. This in turn affected religious literature for the young. There was more concern about actual religious instruction, both for the literate part of the population for whom Watts and others had written, as well as, for the first time, the primarily illiterate working class. The growth of urban industries, particularly in England, had led to the herding together in towns of people for whom the old parochial system was now inadequate. It was for these, and more especially the rural poor in the first place, that the Sunday-school movement developed. Since in this book we are concerned with the home instruction of children, the Sunday-school movement will not be considered here, but it was symptomatic of the general concern for the religious state of the nation which was expressed by many English and American writers in various ways in the late eighteenth and early nineteenth century.

In considering any of the books for children, though they may be written about a variety of different subjects, the religious intention of the authors is frequently very apparent. Religion, and religious knowledge, were things to be discussed and studied and brought into everyday life as a matter of course. In England the tenets of the established religion mainly predominated in the books for children, but there was of course a large nonconformist population as well as a Catholic minority one. Two important societies played a large part in the publication of books for the young, as well as providing tracts for the working classes. These were the Society for Promoting Christian Knowledge, which was founded as early as 1699, and the Religious Tract Society. In America tract societies also proliferated: the New York Tract Society, 1812; the New England Tract Society, 1814; the Philadelphia Female Tract Society, 1816, and so on. Books on history, geography and natural history were among those into which religious matter was inserted and everything was traced back to the Divine Will in a way which is rarely to be found today. Yet in religious writing for the young various contemporary discoveries were reflected, and some of the illustrations to this chapter demonstrate the influence of nineteenth-century archaeological studies, and Biblical studies in particular. Books started to take advantage of wider general knowledge, as in *Palestine for the Young*, published by the Religious Tract Society in 1865, which gave a very accurate description of scenes and customs in the Bible lands. The stories of Joseph and Moses, together with incidents from the life of Christ, had always been especially popular for the young, and these were now illustrated with far greater accuracy of detail. The wider knowledge of Palestine which was brought back and published by travellers, was supplemented by works such as Owen Jones's *Grammar of Ornament*, 1856, which treated of historic styles and was illustrated with lavish examples. Illustrations such as plates 50–54 show the change of style which occurred as a result of this increased concern with detail.

Illustration was always important in religious works for children. Mrs

NEW TESTAMENT. 4

LESSON XIII.

Our SAVIOUR *and the Woman of Samaria.*

PART of the Jewish Rulers were Pharisees and part Sadducees; these two Sects disagreed with each other in some points of Religion, but they all agreed in setting themselves against

E

Opposite:
52 THE CHILD'S COLOURED SCRIPTURE BOOK . . . THE HISTORY OF JOSEPH. G. Routledge & Sons [1867?]. 26 × 23 cm. The story of Joseph was frequently told and illustrated. These chromo-lithographed illustrations were also issued in another version with the text below each picture. The compression of two illustrations on one page is typical of the lack of artistic awareness in the production of many cheaper books for children.

Above:
53 NEW AND COMPREHENSIVE LESSONS CONTAINING A GENERAL OUTLINE OF THE NEW TESTAMENT by Sarah Trimmer. J. Harris & J. Hatchard and Son [1821?]. 14 × 9 cm. The simple woodcuts of this edition of a popular work show the influence of the Neo-classical style.

At this time lived Abraham, a very holy man, who had but one son, Isaac, whom he loved; but God he loved better still. Now to try whether this was true or not, God commanded him to bind his son, as he would a lamb, to sacrifice: to take with him also a knife and wood, that he might make a burnt offering of his son. Good Abraham did it all; travelled with Isaac to the place appointed; bound and laid him on the wood; and just as he raised his arm to slay his child, an angel called from heaven to prevent him. "Abraham," said he, " now know I that thou fearest God, seeing that thou hast not withheld him from thine only son." Then he looked and found a ram in a thicket, which he offered to the Lord, and returned with his son rejoicing.

The children of Israel having lived a great many years in Egypt, there was a new king, who used them cruelly. And God heard their complaints, and commanded Moses to lead them home to Canaan, their own land. But Pharaoh would not let them go. So God brought dreadful plagues upon him, till at last he gladly sent them away.

But Pharaoh pursued them with his army, and overtook them by the Red Sea. Then God commanded the waters to divide, and stand on each side like a wall. So the Israelites passed through the great sea on dry land, but when the Egyptians went to follow, God caused the waves to return to their place, and Pharaoh and his army were all drowned together in the sea, because of their wickedness.

Above:

54 ART PICTURES FROM THE OLD TESTAMENT: SUNDAY READINGS FOR THE YOUNG. Published by the Society for Promoting Christian Knowledge, 1894. 28 × 21 cm. In this book the text is a mere accompaniment to the pictures. The illustrations, by some of the leading artists of the day, were first issued in *Dalziel's Bible Gallery* in 1880.

Above right:

55 PICTURES OF BIBLE HISTORY, WITH SUITABLE DESCRIPTIONS. Hartford, Oliver D. Cooke. 1820. 14 cm. A typical example of the paraphrased Bible stories offered to young children. The large number of illustrations must have made such works very welcome.

ELIEZER AND REBEKAH AT THE WELL. HOLMAN HUNT, DEL.

Sarah Trimmer published her *Series of Prints* in the last years of the eighteenth century especially so that they could be used to adorn the nursery: the accompanying text was published separately, and both sacred and profane history was included in the series. Likewise, 'Robert Burton' (the pseudonym of Nathaniel Crouch) had said of his *Youth's Divine Pastime*, 1729, that it contained 'forty remarkable scripture histories turned into English verse. With forty pictures proper to each story; very delightful for young persons'. In his preface the anonymous author of *The Holy Bible Abridged* wrote not only concerning the illustrations, which he felt would render it more pleasing to children, but also about his reason for writing the work in the first place. The preface is quoted here in full since it was obvious that similar reasons often induced other authors to compile works for the young:

The Author's Design in this Publication is evidently to give Children such a Taste of the Writings of the Holy Pen-man, as may engage them, earnestly and seriously in the Study of the Sacred Books of the *Old* and *New Testament*.

To forward them in this laudable and pious Pursuit, he has selected such Portions of the Scriptures as are both *instructive* and *entertaining*; such as will not only feed the Fancy, but mend the Heart, and establish in the Mind those unalterable Laws of the DEITY, which lead us to the Knowledge of Himself, which cement us together in Society, and on which our Happiness both in this Life and the next must absolutely depend.

To render this little Book the more pleasing to Children, it is embellished with a great Number of Cuts; and, that it may be useful to those more advanced in Years, the Chronology of the most remarkable Events is preserved, and such Notes interspersed as he had Reason to apprehend would be useful.

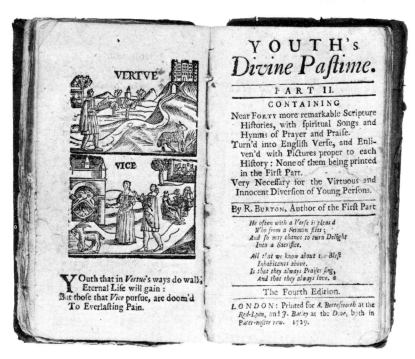

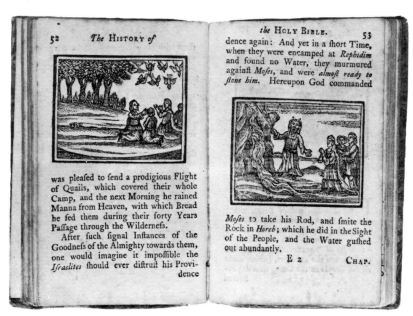

This is the Author's Design, which, he is persuaded, every good *Christian* will approve; and he hopes that he has been careful to execute it in such a Manner, as to spare himself the Pains of an Apology to the Public.

Such a serious-minded approach to the subject, in which this author was typical of many others of the period, changed somewhat under the influence of the more sentimental attitude to children discernible as the nineteenth century progressed. It led to statements like this, from *Fanny and Her Mamma*, 1848:

58 THE PILGRIM'S PROGRESS by John
Bunyan. T. Heptinstall, 1796.
24 × 15 cm. From the time of its
first appearance in the seventeenth
century, this book has been read by
children, although not written for
them. Readers too young to
appreciate its religious allegory
could enjoy it as a great work of
imagination, full of giants and other
strange beings.

Children are our choicest treasures. They are little heirs of immortality, and if it pleases God to commit them to our charge, our first desire should be to train them for heaven. We are not only to rejoice in their happy smiles and in the gladness which their infant voices spread around our home, but we are to remember our responsibility. . . .

We have already mentioned briefly the subject of the observance of Sunday and the importance of Sabbath day literature. Even today, the English Sunday, though fast disappearing under the impact of modern life, still retains some nineteenth-century aspects which mark it out from the day as kept by many continental neighbours. Certain goods are not permitted to be sold on Sundays, and state museums do not open until the afternoon, thus permitting all who so wish to attend divine service first. The Puritans in England and America had been very strict in their observance of the Sabbath, but in spite of laws remaining on the statute book, matters had become lax during the eighteenth century. But by the end of the century reformers were at work to improve the religious and moral standards of the community, and the result can be seen in the nineteenth-century children's books. In the middle- and upper-class households with whose children this book is primarily concerned, the conformists kept the Sabbath strictly. For the younger members of the family it could be a day to endure rather than to enjoy, since play was not permitted (except perhaps with a Noah's Ark). Going to church, learning texts, reading and discussing the Bible: these filled the child's Sunday. On the other hand, it could, in some families, mean that the children spent more of the day with their parents, and less in the nursery than was customary on week days. In the opening chapter of *Sunday Afternoons with Mamma*, 1866, published by the Religious Tract Society, the Sabbath was described as follows:

Sunday was a happy day to little Kate and Ernest. Shall I tell you how they spent it? On Saturday evening, just before bed-time, they always helped their nurse to put away in the nursery cupboard all their toys and their 'week day' Picture Books, and then from a drawer below was taken, first a box of moveable letters, which Kate and Ernest (or Erny as he was usually called) were only allowed to use on Sunday.

The children were very fond of putting these letters together so as to form words, and they often were able to spell a verse from the Bible in this way.

But besides the letter box, in the Sunday drawer were kept two large Picture Books, with large coloured pictures of Bible scenes. One of these belonged to Katie, and the other to Erny, and there were some smaller books as well, with pretty Bible stories, and sweet hymns in them. All these were taken out of the drawer on Saturday night, and put away again on Sunday night, because if Katie and Erny had had these letters and books every day, they would, perhaps, have grown tired of them, and would have had no fresh books for Sunday.

59 SUNDAY AFTERNOONS IN THE
NURSERY; OR, FAMILIAR NARRATIVES
FROM THE BOOK OF GENESIS by Maria
Louisa Charlesworth. Seeley,
Jackson, and Halliday, 1866.
15 × 12 cm. The sort of scene
envisaged in many of the books
discussed in the present work, with a
group of children gathered round a
mother or other relative.

Then dear mamma always tried to make Sunday a very happy day
to her children; and when they were not happy, I think it must have
been either when they were not very well, or not very good.

In the morning they went to the house of God with their papa and
mamma. . . .

But there was another Sunday occupation which was permissible: reading
books – of the right sort. Undoubtedly the most famous book to come into
this category was *The Pilgrim's Progress*. This had been children's reading
from the time it was first published in 1678, though often in an adapted or
abridged form: *Bunyan Explained to a Child* (2ed 1825) was a version by the
Rev Isaac Taylor. But there were a great many writers for children who
provided religious instruction under the guise of stories or short novels,
which might be considered as permitted Sunday reading. Among them was
Sarah Smith ('Hesba Stretton'): her books such as *Jessica's First Prayer* and
Alone in London, were frequently reprinted.

Certain works maintained their popularity throughout all the changes
that occurred between their first appearance in print and the end of the
nineteenth century. Isaac Watts's poems continued to be published and
learnt. When Lewis Carroll parodied two of them in *Alice* as 'How doth the
little crocodile' and 'Twas the voice of the lobster', he could do so knowing
that the originals were perfectly familiar to his young readers. Another
work that continued to be published was *Hymns in Prose for Children* by Mrs
Barbauld, which first appeared in London in 1781 and in Norwich (Conn.)
in 1786. In 1865 John Murray published an excellent High Victorian
version of this work, in which text and illustrations were attractively

59

blended on the page. The editor of the 1865 text was conscious of the illustrative quality of the work, and wrote in the preface:

> The varied and picturesque descriptions with which the continuous thread of argument is strung, render the task of illustration at once easy and suggestive.
>
> Few works could be found which challenge the pencil and fancy of the artist in a greater degree; and it is hoped the present effort may be deemed worthy of the text.
>
> The blending of the illustrations with the type will be found no unimportant feature; a unity being thereby obtained, which is alike pleasing and less fatiguing both to the mind and eye, a matter of some importance with the young.

After this, it comes as something of a surprise to read in Mrs Barbauld's preface, following some remarks on Dr Watts and 'the condescension of his muse', such words as:

> But it may well be doubted whether poetry ought to be lowered to the capacities of children, or whether they should not rather be kept from reading verse till they are able to relish good verse; for the very essence of poetry is an elevation in thought and style above the common standard; and if it wants this character, it wants all that renders it valuable.'

In many of these early children's books, there appears to be a pre-occupation with death – often a lingering one too. This may in part be for the better pointing of the tale, giving time for a reformation to be effected or pious examples to be fully appreciated. On the other hand, we are reminded that death was common in the lives of the young children about whom we read, and in many stories we hear of the mother losing her child or the child his or her parent. We should remember this when in a work like *Peep of Day*, 1868, we find the following passage:

> When a little child, who loves God, falls sick, and is going to die, God says to the angels, 'Go and fetch that little child's soul up to heaven.'[1] Then the angels fly down, the little darling shuts its eyes, it lays its head on its mother's bosom, its breath stops; – the child is dead. Where is its soul? the angels are carrying it up to heaven.
>
> How happy the child is now! Its pain is over; it is grown quite good;[2] it is bright like an angel.[3] It holds a harp in its hand, and begins to sing

HYMNS IN PROSE

FOR

CHILDREN.

BY MRS. BARBAULD.

PHILADELPHIA:
PRINTED BY BENJAMIN JOHNSON,
No. 31, MARKET STREET.

1806.

60 HYMNS IN PROSE FOR CHILDREN by Mrs Barbauld. Philadelphia, B. Johnson, 1806. 14 cm. This work, popular in England for over a century after its publication in 1781, was soon published in America where it was also frequently re-issued and illustrated.

---

[1] 'And it came to pass that the beggar died, and was carried by angels into Abraham's bosom.' Luke xvi. 22.

[2] 'The *spirits* of just men made *perfect*.' Heb. xii. 23.

[3] 'Then shall the righteous shine forth as the sun in the kingdom of their Father.' Matt. xiii. 43.

[4] 'I heard the voice of harpers harping with their harps. These were redeemed from among men.' Rev. xiv. 2, 4.

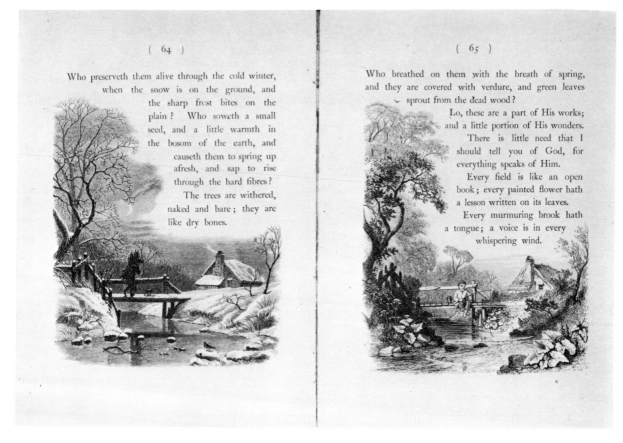

Who preserveth them alive through the cold winter, when the snow is on the ground, and the sharp frost bites on the plain? Who soweth a small seed, and a little warmth in the bosom of the earth, and causeth them to spring up afresh, and sap to rise through the hard fibres?

The trees are withered, naked and bare; they are like dry bones.

Who breathed on them with the breath of spring, and they are covered with verdure, and green leaves sprout from the dead wood?

Lo, these are a part of His works; and a little portion of His wonders.

There is little need that I should tell you of God, for everything speaks of Him.

Every field is like an open book; every painted flower hath a lesson written on its leaves.

Every murmuring brook hath a tongue; a voice is in every whispering wind.

a sweet song of praise to God.[4] Its little body is put into a grave, and turns into dust. One day God will make its body alive again.

A preoccupation with death is only one of the many characteristics of the religious instruction books which make them so different from their modern counterparts. In the first place far more were published than today. In the Victorian period few middle- or upper-class children would have passed through childhood without having read one or more of this type of book. Today, religious books of any kind are hardly read out of school, particularly in those very countries where religious instruction was formerly so predominant, namely England and America. In the United States the nineteenth century saw the immigration of large numbers of people whose background and religious beliefs varied considerably; the imposition of one particular interpretation would have been contrary to that liberty of conscience which many of them had sought in the States. In England, the state church experienced the controversies of 'high' and 'low' churchmen, and some people also began to admit the existence of other forms of the Christian faith – and even, reluctantly, of other faiths. The nineteenth

61 HYMNS IN PROSE FOR CHILDREN by A. L. Barbauld. J. Murray, 1865. 19 × 14 cm. A good example of the high standard of book design reached during the 1860s, in which text and pictures were happily related. This opening shows the same scene in winter and summer.

century also saw the advent of Catholic emancipation in England and the
admission of Jews to normal rights of citizenship. In spite of much new
church building, there began the slow decline in importance of religion in
the social life of Britain. Nevertheless, at the end of our period the style of
religious instruction, almost everywhere, was far less different from that
at the beginning of this survey than the subsequent fifty years were to bring
about.

Minorities always tend to cling more strongly to their beliefs, and which-
ever faith found itself in that position always ensured that its young should
be well imbued with the traditional forms of its own beliefs. In countries
where religious bodies, particularly the Catholic Church, have continued
to take responsibility for education, something of the nineteenth century
style of juvenile reading prevails, while regular attendance at Mass ensures
an equally regular programme of instruction.

Surveying our period as a whole the subtle change in religious books
published for children is quite observable. Earlier centuries made little
concession to the child's abilities or proclivities, and in some communities
in both England and America his religious instruction was stark and
severe. The more tolerant eighteenth century tended to concentrate on
formal observances, while the nineteenth century brought religion back
into daily life again, just at a time when scientific developments were
beginning to sow seeds of doubt in many intellectual minds. Doubt certainly never permeated religious writings for children. Nevertheless, we
become conscious, as the century progresses, of a decidedly secular influence
at work, in spite of the publication of missionary journeys and archaeological discoveries which resulted in attempts to give more accurate back-
grounds, in time and area, to descriptions of the life of Christ. Eventually
children could be offered tales, and even natural history books, which
would make no mention of the Creator – something rarely to be found in
the earlier period.

Remarkably enough, of all the subjects discussed in this book, it is in the
field of religious illustration that we find the least change in modern works
from those considered in this survey – many today still have a slightly
old-fashioned air about them. Perhaps the greatest change we have seen
in this century, when formal religion has come to play so small a part in the
child's life, is the fact that children are told of the existence of faiths other
than their own. This would have been unthinkable for the writers we have
discussed in this chapter, who wrote so often of the benefits of Christianity
being brought to the 'heathen'.

Cheerfulness

...ce paid no attention to her advice;
...dily siezed a large piece of turnip,
...he carried to his mouth: as might
...een expected, he burnt his tongue
...; and instantly screamed aloud.
...her did not suffer him to remain at
...but took him away, and put him
...ack room, and there left him.

...you perceive, my young friends,
...ce was no gainer by his frowardness,
...was not only deprived of the use
...tongue for some time, but he lost
... dinner, and was shut up in a back

W. BELCH's Life of WILLIAM the 4th.

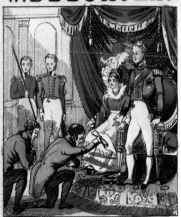

1

William the 4th. ascends the Throne,

To rule a grateful nation,

Bids trade & commerce flourish round,

From his exalted station.

2

At Brighton's famed Pavillion he,

Deigns to take his abode,

Makes his triumphant entry,

While numbers throng the road.

Le lendemain 6 mai, elle s'empara de la bastille des Augustins. Le samedi 7, de grand matin, l'attaque de la bastille des Tournelles commença. Jeanne, descendue dans le fossé, dressait une échelle contre le parapet, lorsqu'un trait d'arbalète la perça de part en part entre le cou et l'épaule. Elle arracha le fer de la plaie; on lui offrit alors de *charmer* la blessure, elle s'y refusa, disant « qu'elle aimerait mieux mourir que rien faire qui fût contre la volonté de Dieu ». Elle se confessa et pria longuement pendant que ses troupes se reposaient. Puis donnant l'ordre de recommencer l'assaut, elle se jeta au plus fort du combat, criant aux assaillants : « Tout est vôtre, entrez-y! »

La bastille fut prise, et tous les défenseurs périrent. Il ne restait plus un Anglais sur la rive gauche de la Loire.

pag. 232

TEUTONIA

Deutschlands wichtigste Ereignisse und das Leben seiner berühmtesten Männer, in leichtfasslichen Erzählungen für die Jugend dargestellt von E. MAUKISCH.

pag. 83

Fortsetzung der Germania.

Berlin, Verlag von Winckelmann u. Söhne.

6 Moral Improvement

This is perhaps the most difficult subject to define, not through lack of material but rather through an excess. Before the middle of the nineteenth century almost all books had either a religious or moral content – and frequently both. Every aspect of the didactic output for children could be comprehended in those two words; even when the ostensible subject was geography, or history, or grammar, the text could be made to serve the purpose of the religious or moral educator. Religion and morals were so inextricably mixed that it might be as well to define the difference. Religious instruction could be allied to the teachings of a particular church, or merely indicate the omnipresence of an omniscient deity. Moral instruction can, of course, exist independently of religion, though in the nineteenth century this was unusual – even *Twelve Cents Worth of Wit*, 1795, insists it is 'for little folks of all denominations'. But the writer's concern for right and wrong, virtue and vice, could (and often did) degenerate into mere rules of behaviour, and in particular such behaviour as would not only be acceptable in polite society, but which might also be expected to bring material benefits in its train. The same trend can be studied in the early copybooks.[1] In these, the pious texts and Biblical quotations typical of seventeenth-

[1] *English handwriting, 1540 – 1853,* by J. I. Whalley, 1969.

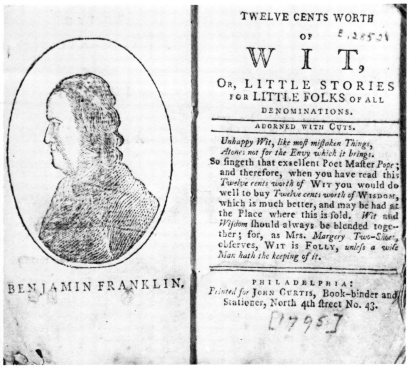

Opposite top:
66 JEANNE D'ARC par M. Boutet de Monvel. Paris, E. Plon, Nourrit & Cie [1896]. 23 × 31 cm. One of the many delicate coloured works produced by this artist towards the end of the nineteenth century, some of them dealing with various aspects of French life, such as national songs, or, as here, history.

Opposite bottom:
67 TEUTONIA: DEUTSCHLANDS WICHTIGSTE EREIGNISSE UND DAS LEBEN SEINER BERÜHMTESTEN MÄNNER LEICHT FASSLICHEN ERZÄHLUNGEN FÜR DIE JUGEND (Teutonia: Germany's Most Important Events and the Lives of its Most Famous Men, Told in Easy Tales for the Young) by E. Maukisch, Berlin [c. 1850]. 18 × 13 cm. One of many books produced in Germany, England, and elsewhere which presented history in the form of the lives of great men. As so often in German books of this period, the pictures are few and the text fairly solid. The illustration shows the engraved frontispiece and title-page, both hand-coloured.

Left:
68 TWELVE CENTS WORTH OF WIT; OR, LITTLE STORIES FOR LITTLE FOLKS OF ALL DENOMINATIONS. Philadelphia, John Curtis [c. 1795]. 10 cm. The American edition of a book published by John Newbery entitled *Six Pennyworth of Wit*, but otherwise identical.

69 THE LIFE AND ADVENTURES OF
ROBINSON CRUSOE by Daniel Defoe.
Philadelphia, Key & Mielke, 1831.
First published in 1719, the story of
Robinson Crusoe was soon adopted
by young readers. It was translated
and imitated in a number of
countries, and also inspired much
moral reflection. Abridged editions
are still read by children and books
based on its 'desert-island' theme
continue to enchant them.

Bottom:

70 JEMIMA PLACID; OR, THE
ADVANTAGES OF GOOD NATURE,
EXEMPLIFIED IN A SERIES OF FAMILIAR
INCIDENTS [by M. J. Kilner]. 3ed.
John Marshall 1786. 12 × 8 cm.
Although written with a moral
purpose, this was a book which
concentrated on social behaviour in
a way very characteristic of the
eighteenth century. The text and
illustration shown here were meant
to show the effect of irrational fears,
impetuosity and thoughtlessness.

century examples were gradually superseded in the eighteenth century by
moral maxims with materialistic overtones, usually indicating that the
practice of virtue would invariably bring temporal rewards. Since this was
no more true then than now, many a morally upright youth must have had
to content himself with another much publicized maxim, namely that virtue
was its own reward. This chapter is not greatly concerned with the moral
tale presented in the form of leisure reading, but rather with those works
whose moral tone was intentionally didactic. It is a very fine distinction,
but one that must be made if the chapter is not to include a study of almost
all works written for children over a period of more than two hundred

years. A study of moral improvement writings reveals much that explains the general social character of the 200 years under consideration. No doubt much of the popularity of a work like *Robinson Crusoe* (from the adult point of view anyway!) lay in the strong non-conformist, self-reliant moral attitude of the eponymous hero.

'To fortify the heart with virtue, while we are leading Children through the paths of learning, is an object parents and tutors should never lose sight of.' So ran the preface 'To Parents and Tutors' in a work entitled *Tea-table Dialogues between a Governess and Mary Sensible, Eliza Thoughtful, . . . Lucy Lively and Emma Tempest*, published in 1779. In this book we have before us two important aspects of moral instruction: first, the idea that it could and should be introduced into all fields of education; secondly, we have an example of one method of making it memorable, and if possible palatable. Personification was a much-favoured means of achieving this, and so we find a procession of people like Tommy Playlove, Jacky Lovebook, Jemima Placid, Harry Fairborn and Master Trueworth, passing across the years for the edification of juvenile readers. The old-fashioned sins, such as pride and gluttony, were well supplemented by what we may call the behavioural and social sins: disobedience, rudeness, selfishness, cruelty and such like. Towards the end of the eighteenth century the earlier concepts of a 'godly, righteous and sober life', or 'seen and not heard', and of proper social behaviour, became modified under the influence of Rousseau and his English imitators. There was less conviction that all children were inherently evil and more pre-occupation with 'natural' virtue. Naughtiness, however, could never go unpunished – at least in books. There were a few exceptions to this general rule, and Catherine Sinclair's *Holiday House*, 1839, was one of them, showing children as 'noisy, frolicsome, mischievous'. On the whole, even the least slip into thoughtlessness seems to have been considered worthy of retribution; moreover, it was often made to appear so natural a concomitant to bad behaviour, that many a child must have been surprised to discover that the heavens did not in fact immediately retaliate on the commission of some forbidden deed. The aim of the conscientious parent and educator was goodness rather than happiness for the child (happiness would come with virtue), together with the desire to inculcate a code of righteous behaviour that would enable the child to take his place successfully in the adult world. In such a scheme suitable chosen books could play an important part:

> The books read by the little tenants of the nursery, assist, no doubt, in forming their matured characters: consequently, the task of writing for very young children is one of the utmost importance; and those who undertake it, should never lose sight of the one great object, – which is, to plant, and to promote the growth of moral principles in the youthful mind.

says 'Solomon Lovechild' in *Little Tales for the Nursery*, and few indeed were

Where I see the blind or lame,
   Deaf or dumb, I'll kindly treat them:
I deserve to feel the same,
   If I mock, or hurt, or cheat them.

If I meet with railing tongues,
   Why should I return them railing,
Since I best revenge my wrongs
   By my patience never failing?

When I hear them telling lies,
   Talking foolish, cursing, swearing,
First I'll try to make them wise,
   Or I'll soon go out of hearing.

106

What though I be low or mean,
   I'll engage the rich to love me,
While I'm modest, neat, and clean,
   And submit when they reprove me.

If I should be poor and sick,
   I shall meet, I hope, with pity;
Since I love to help the weak,
   Though they're neither fair nor witty.

107

71 DIVINE AND MORAL SONGS FOR CHILDREN by Isaac Watts. Sampson Low, Son & Marston, 1866 [1865]. 20 × 15 cm. 'Good Resolutions' was one of the moral poems first published in 1740 as an addition to the *Divine Songs* of 1715. Watts's work had a very long life and was still being reprinted throughout the nineteenth century. The poem is shown here in a mid-Victorian setting with illustrations by W. Small. Other artists contributed illustrations to the rest of the book.

the writers who forgot this object, at least up to the middle of the nineteenth century.

All these books reveal the image of life and society as our forebears felt it should be. It was in the moral sphere above all that the adult believed he was able to mould the world to his liking, by indicating moral standards and by framing codes of conduct for the benefit of the next generation. On the whole both morals and conduct were largely those of the middle class, its members hopefully aping the class above, to which wealth might give them access, and anxious to impress on working people a proper appreciation of their own lower position in society. That this was no new idea in Victorian England we may see from one of Isaac Watts's *Moral Songs*, first 71 published in 1740, and constantly reprinted; it is shown here in a mid-Victorian illustrated version, where it is equally at home.

The titles of many of the moral instruction books are themselves instructive, since they provide clear evidence of the contemporary attitude to the child and his reading. The titles were meant to encourage purchase of the books, by indicating the contents within. Would some of these popular titles sell a book today, or even fifty years ago? There are many titles to chose from, and only a few can be quoted here. Among works which went into many editions were: *The Young Moralist, Consisting of Allegorical and Entertaining Essays in Prose and Verse*, by G. Wright (fourth edition London 1792); *The Blossoms of Morality* (London 1789 and Philadelphia 1795), 76 which may have owed some of its popularity to the illustrations by John Bewick with which it was adorned; *The Brother's Gift; or, the Naughty Girl*

68

Oubli des injures

Héroisme de l'Amitié.

Trait extraordinaire de générosité.

Reformed (London 1773, Worcester, USA, 1786); and *The Triumph of Good Nature Exhibited in the History of Master Henry Fairborn and Master Trueworth* (London *c.* 1801, Boston 1804). The list could go on for pages and can be mirrored in similar French and German lists: *L'Enfance Eclairé; ou, Les Virtus et les Vices,* 1813; *Contes Moraux pour la Jeunesse, c.* 1845; and the works of writers like Franz Hoffmann, whose *Hundertundfünfzig Moralische Erzählungen für Kleine Kinder,* 1848, also went into numerous editions. In many such works the intention was to convey moral instruction by means of noble examples, as we see in *La Morale Enseignée par l'Example,* 1810, and other similar writings.

But perhaps the most common way of instilling both moral and social behaviour was by means of the fable, which, twisted, mutilated or 'arranged', was everywhere considered singularly appropriate for this type of instruction throughout our whole period. The fable has a long history – probably a more continuous one than any existing religious faith. In the West it is particularly associated with the name of Æsop, but similar compilations come from outside Europe, including the Near and Far East. As most commonly employed, it consisted of a short tale in which a certain line of conduct was portrayed, together with its consequences; the participants in such tales were usually animals who thus found themselves involved in situations which could be paralleled in human experience; in case the reader should fail to grasp the point, a moral was appended to make the relevance quite clear. But fables, as some serious writers began to perceive, had one important defect: they were not true. It appeared highly immoral to these authors that such a deceit should be practised on the young at whom they were specifically aimed. The indefatigable 'Mrs Teachwell' (Lady Fenn), faced this fact and dealt with it in her own way in *Morals to a Set of Fables . . . The Morals in Dialogues, Between a Mother and Children, In two parts,* 1783:

Left:
72 MORALS TO A SET OF FABLES, by Mrs Teachwell. John Marshall (1783). 16 × 10 cm. Here it is clearly pointed out to William that the fable is only meant to teach a lesson, and not to be taken literally. The artist appears to have had some difficulty with the relative size of the insects and the background against which they are set!

Above:
73 LA MORALE ENSEIGNÉE PAR L'EXEMPLE; OU, CHOIX D'ANECDOTES, TRAITS HISTORIQUES, MOTS REMARQUABLES ET PETITES HISTOIRES, POUR L'INSTRUCTION ET L'AMUSEMENT DE LA JEUNESSE (Moral Behaviour Taught by Example; or, a Choice of Anecdotes, Historic Deeds, Remarkable Sayings and Short Stories, for the Instruction and Amusement of Youth). 5ed. Paris, 1810. 16 × 10 cm. A selection of stories about noble deeds designed to encourage emulation by young readers.

34   WILLIAM's MORALS to

MAM-MA.

That Fa-ble is to teach you, that it is bet-ter to work, than to do no-thing but play.

FABLES in MONOSYLLABLES.   35

WIL-LI-AM.

Mam-ma! the Fox got the meat from the Crow --- should he?

MAM-MA.

The Fox was a thief; but if the Crow had not been so fil-ly as to think her-self a-ble to sing, she might have kept her meat.

WIL-LI-AM.

C 2   GEORGE's

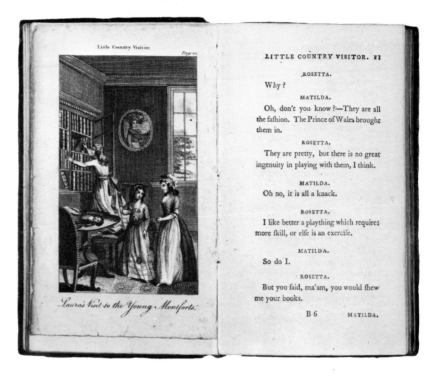

Laura's Visit to the Young Montforts.

LITTLE COUNTRY VISITOR. 11

ROSETTA.

Why?

MATILDA.

Oh, don't you know?—They are all
the fashion. The Prince of Wales brought
them in.

ROSETTA.

They are pretty, but there is no great
ingenuity in playing with them, I think.

MATILDA.

Oh no, it is all a knack.

ROSETTA.

I like better a plaything which requires
more skill, or else is an exercise.

MATILDA.

So do I.

ROSETTA.

But you said, ma'am, you would shew
me your books.

B 6　　　　MATILDA.

Top:

74 DRAMATIC DIALOGUES FOR THE USE
OF YOUNG PERSONS [by Mrs
Pinchard]. Vol. II. E. Newbery,
1792. 17 × 10 cm. *The Little Country
Visitor* was one of a series of playlets
which tried to exemplify moral
virtues in dramatic form. The
sophisticated town-bred children are
shown at a disadvantage compared
with the more 'natural' country
visitor. One of the children is
playing with a 'bandalore' (the
modern yo-yo). A version was
published in Boston in 1798.

Bottom:

75 THE LILLIPUTIAN AUCTION, TO
WHICH ALL LITTLE MASTERS AND
MISSES ARE INVITED BY CHARLY
CHATTER. T. Carnan, 1777.
10 × 6 cm. A method of making a
moral point, in which objects act as
a 'cover' for moral virtues. The 'lots'
are then sold to those most in need of
them. 'The receipt to make young
ladies beautiful' which was concealed
in the packet shown here proved to
be 'good humour'; it was bought by
Miss Surly!

12 *The* LILLIPUTIAN AUCTION.

his promising not to repeat his Fault;
and, at the same Time, his Sincerity
was greatly applauded. He was so
overjoyed upon regaining his Papa's
Favour, that, seeing a Beggar Woman
before the Door, he flew to her,
like Lightning, and gave her a Shilling, which was all the Money he
had. As soon as he looked into this
Glass, he found himself as beautiful
as an Angel.—Who'll buy this excellent Glass?

Master *Froward.* Not I. I have
no Occasion for it, for I have no
Faults to be told of; and if I had, I
should not like to be told of them.

Master *Affable.* Indeed, Master
Froward, you have great Occasion
for it; so I'll buy it myself, and
make you a Present of it.

　　　　Knock'd down.

　　　LOT

The LILLIPUTIAN AUCTION. 13

LOT 2.

A PACKET.

*Which contains a Receipt to make
young Ladies beautiful.*

UPON the putting up this Lot, all
the young Ladies immediately
crouded about the little Auctioneer,
　　　　　　　　　　—except

There must always remain one accusation against Fables, namely,
Falsehood; but surely it is easily explained to the children, that it is but
their own usual favorite sport of '*making believe*', as they call feigning
visits, trading, *&c. &c.* with no design to deceive; yet, to guard
against the shadow of evil, I have been explicit on that point in some
of the dialogues; lest the little books should fall into the hands of any
poor friendless child, and lessen his regard to truth.

70

Nevertheless, in spite of such a severe handicap the fable remained a popular method of instruction – a means to inculcate virtue, explain behaviour, and show the result of foolish or evil deeds. Moreover, such tales readily lent themselves to illustration, and if the child was to be encouraged to learn by the aid of pictures the fable thus had an added advantage – especially since most printers could produce more or less suitable pictures from stock.

On the whole, writings for moral instruction were not so well illustrated as other didactic works; even some of the most popular works, such as those by the influential Maria Edgeworth, were frequently issued with unrelieved text. This was no doubt partly because the subject matter was so diffuse, and had no point of concentration such as it had in other fields. Since many of the moral instruction works related either to everyday happenings or to the animal world, there was less need for the publisher to be specific in his illustrative material. It has always been difficult suitably to portray greed, pride, envy, sloth – and perhaps even less easy to illustrate generosity, good nature, patience, diligence, and all the other good qualities which the persevering parent or governess attempted to instil into the reluctant child. Various attempts were made to bring these abstract qualities within the appreciation of even small children by relating them directly to the child's own experience. Hence a whole crop of 'awful warning' tales, in which that arch-sin of the nursery, disobedience, played such a large part. Other methods might be used to involve the child such as we find in *Dramatic Dialogues for the Use of Young Persons*, by Mrs Pinchard, published by E. Newbery in 1792 or *The Lilliputian Auction*, by 'Charly Chatter', published by T. Carnan in 1777. The latter, which makes use of the following device: 'Lot 2: A packet which contains a receipt to make young ladies beautiful' – and which, when opened, contains the couplet:

'If beautiful you wou'd appear,
Always be good humour'd dear.'

This work had two well-known successors, one of which, *The Toilet*, 1821, is particularly famous; the other was the boys' equivalent, *A Suit of Armour for Youth*, 1824. In these two, illustrations could be transformed by the lifting of a flap, to reveal the appropriate moral quality written underneath.

Although the need to educate the child in moral values and social behaviour did not lessen as the nineteenth century progressed, it had rivals in all the other subjects that now claimed the child's attention. Education had become a more serious and ordered business. Moral and religious instruction, which had been the most important items in the eighteenth-century nursery, now competed with a whole world of practical information which it was considered necessary for the child to know even before his days of formal schooling commenced.

If we judged only by the conversations reproduced in books, the children who underwent this training must have been insufferable prigs. Although

71

76 THE BLOSSOMS OF MORALITY.
Intended for the amusement and
instruction of young ladies and
gentlemen. By the editor of *The
Looking-Glass for the Mind*. With . . .
cuts designed and engraved by
J. Bewick. Printed for E. Newbery,
1796. 17 × 10 cm. An interesting
comment on the period is that a book
of this kind could be offered 'for the
amusement . . . of young ladies and
gentlemen'. The Bewick brothers,
Thomas and John, greatly improved
the standard of book illustration in
both adults' and children's books.
John Bewick illustrated the Abbé
Berquin's work *L'Ami des Enfans*,
which, as quoted in the title above,
was translated into English as *The
Looking-Glass for the Mind*.

writers occasionally allowed themselves a little sympathy for the youthful
wrong-doer, he (or she) must *always* see the error of his ways before the end
of the tale. One of the most charmingly naughty children was Maria
Edgeworth's Rosamond, especially in the famous tale of *The Purple Jar*,
but she was made to suffer most cruelly (we feel) for youthful errors of
judgment. Given the choice between a new pair of shoes and a 'purple'
jar she chose the latter. Her lack of shoes prevented her joining subsequent
family activities, while the 'purple' jar proved to be only a white jar containing a purple liquid. All of which her mother let her find out for herself
in order to emphasize the lesson! More typical of the children we meet was
Jemima Placid, in whom we see 'the advantages of good nature exemplified
in a variety of familiar incidents'; or little George, who remarks smugly
that when he was offered bread and butter he refused it because he knew he
was not allowed to eat butter (he rather spoilt the effect by adding that his
aunt heard about this example of his goodness and obedience, and rewarded
him with cake!). Then there was Camillus, whose response to his father's
instruction was typical of much of the high-flown dialogue put into the
mouths of children:

Sir W. T. Well, Camillus, how do you find yourself this morning after our conversation of yesterday?

Camillus. Indeed my mind, I am sure, is much the better for it, as the fable which you read to me made me think all the time I was going through the shrubbery, what I should do without you to help me, as the Laurel did the poor honeysuckle, when it found how weak it was in the storm.

Sir W. T. Your reflection, my good boy, is very just; and as long as you will depend upon my assistance in all the storms of life, as well as the sunshine (which you may find often will dazzle and blind you for a time), you may be sure of my utmost efforts to be of use to you.

This is taken from *Entertaining Instructions, in a Series of Familiar Dialogues Between a Parent and his Children, Interspersed with Original Fables*, 1805; moreover, horrid little Camillus was perpetually insisting that his sister should also benefit from these 'entertaining instructions'. It is interesting to notice the complete change of attitude to this type of moral instruction which occurred during the nineteenth century. About ninety years after Camillus and his father had enjoyed their improving talks, in an advertisement at the end of an English edition of a universal old favourite, *The Basket of Flowers* (by J. C. von Schmid), a certain book was recommended as being morally suitable with the advantage that it was 'without any "preaching" or "goody-goodyism"'. What a change in attitude from *The Blossoms of Morality* or *The Young Moralist* at the beginning of the century!

In all these moral works, both those overtly didactic and those meant to instruct by means of fables or other stories, there was little imagination or humour, two qualities which the mid-nineteenth century was to supply. In doing so the accepted moral code was frequently turned up-side down, as we find in *Alice*. Perhaps equally important in showing the gradual change which was to come over the moral and behavioural books, was the publication of Heinrich Hoffmann's *Struwwelpeter*, which first appeared in England in 1848. Hoffmann points out the result of disobedience and other moral failures, but it is his amateurish drawings and caricatured events which distinguish his work compared to the solemn warnings to which contemporary children had become accustomed. *The English Struwwelpeter (Shock-headed Peter)* went into many editions like its continental counterpart, and spawned many imitators. Later works, like *The Little Minxes* and *The Young Ragamuffins*, not only copied Hoffmann's slightly archaic style of illustration but also indicated a much more lenient attitude to the faults of childhood – at least on the part of the more-indulgent adult. But such books were not meant primarily as didactic works, though they commenced a tradition which, passing through Hilaire Belloc and others, leads to our own day – 'turning un-morality into a kind of inverted moral laughter' as Darton says. But the moral tale still continued its sober way, and indeed, well after *Struwwelpeter* and almost contemporary with *Alice* came two very moral

77 ALICE'S ADVENTURES IN WONDERLAND by Lewis Carroll. With illustrations by John Tenniel. Twenty-third thousand. Macmillan & Co., 1870. 18 × 13 cm. First published in 1866, *Alice* was a milestone in juvenile literature, turning accepted standards and knowledge upside-down in a way that has continued to attract adult as well as young readers.

ladies whose existence continues to warn many children today. These were Mrs Doasyouwouldbedoneby and Mrs Bedonebyasyoudid from *The Water-Babies* by Charles Kingsley, published in 1863.

But by the last quarter of the nineteenth century, the advent of universal primary education in most western countries showed up the necessity of revising the ideas of moral and social behaviour, which for so long had been considered suitable in a settled middle-class society possessed of a highly commercial outlook. Exactly what alternative ideas should take their place, and how they should be conveyed to the young, is a subject that has continued to occupy educationalists ever since.

1. SHOCK-HEADED PETER.

Just look at him! There he stands,
With his nasty hair and hands.
See! his nails are never cut;
They are grim'd as black as soot;
And the sloven, I declare,
Never once has comb'd his hair;
Any thing to me is sweeter
Than to see Shock-headed Peter.

('2')

78 THE ENGLISH STRUWWELPETER; OR, PRETTY STORIES AND FUNNY PICTURES FOR LITTLE CHILDREN by Heinrich Hoffmann. 20th edition after the 80th German edition. Frankfurt a/M. printed, sold by W. Mogg [1865?]. This work followed the pattern set by other 'awful warning' books, but carried both the pictures and the verses over into the ridiculous. Indeed, ridicule must have been the reaction of many children when confronted with some of the more ponderous moral and behavioural tales of the period. The original illustrations are hand-coloured; the book was first published in English in 1848, with a slightly different version of 'Shock-headed Peter'.

7 History

The study of history was one of the most popular subjects among educationalists. As we have seen in an earlier chapter, it was highly recommended as suitable to produce in the mind of the young reader a true appreciation of vice and virtue, reward and punishment – provided, of course, that the incidents were carefully chosen. In an age when 'education' meant, for most people, classical education, history meant the history of the Greeks and Romans. The study of national histories came later and in the beginning, showed little of the concern for accuracy or first-hand contacts with original sources that can be noted in the study of classical history. Latin and Greek writers were quoted or adapted for the juvenile reader, but national histories tended to rely on brief facts or, equally, on popular, long-established legend. Although many writers expressed a concern in their prefaces for the capabilities of the young, this was far less apparent in the indigestible texts that followed. Perhaps the biggest change we have seen in the present century (though its beginnings can be traced earlier) is the idea that history is more than a catalogue of kings and wars, and that the lives of ordinary people are also the concern of the historian. Titles like *Everyday life in* . . . give a completely different picture of the past from the one absorbed by previous generations of children.

As with other subjects in the eighteenth and nineteenth centuries, history for home reading was also presented by means of the conversational method, though here too the 'conversation' was more a series of lectures punctuated by leading questions. The dates of kings, queens and presidents, were the most important facts for the child to absorb as far as the history of his own country was concerned, and such facts were easily associated with rhymes which attempted to compress the main events of a reign or a life into four memorable rhyming couplets – with extraordinary results. To aid the memorizing of this essential framework of history a series of portraits was frequently supplied. But, as in so many children's books, the illustrations were very crude, one sovereign looking very much like another, so that the portraits can scarcely have produced the effect desired.

But there was no doubt in the minds of the educators that carefully selected history stories could be used for moral purposes, and that the main study must be devoted to the lives of great personages. The world, therefore, became divided into good rulers and bad rulers, with the addition, in Britain at least, of a strong Protestant bias. The good must be rewarded and the bad punished, clearly and unequivocally, a result not necessarily consistent with historical truth. In spite of statements to the contrary, there was not much real attempt to adapt to childish abilities, and some works intended for quite young readers lived up to the opinion of the mouse in *Alice's Adventures in Wonderland* who offered his tale of 'William the Conqueror whose cause was favoured by the Pope . . .' as an example of 'the driest thing I know'. It is interesting to note that even in these outspoken days there are certain aspects of life which some parents do not choose to thrust before very young children, but of which our ancestors

79 A COMPENDIOUS HISTORY OF ENGLAND FROM THE INVASION BY THE ROMANS TO THE WAR WITH FRANCE IN MDCCXCIV. G. G. & J. Robinson. 1794. 16 × 9 cm. An early illustrated history book for the young, the title-page stating that the cuts are by John and Thomas Bewick. Stiff (and imaginary) portraits of sovereigns are accompanied by brief rhyming descriptions of the main events in each reign. These were really only a kind of *aide-memoire*, since full prose accounts were also supplied.

Canute, Danish King of England.

Then DANISH Invaders came over the main,
And the kings were, in turn, ANGLO-SAXON and DANE.

CANUTE THE DANE

...rageous flattery from those about them. Some of Canute's silly
...rtiers sought on one occasion to recommend themselves to their

wrote with never a blush: Edward IV and Jane Shore or the wayward lives of Anne Boleyn and Catherine Howard.

In addition to all this solid fare there was always in every country a leavening of folk history. Sometimes the subject matter was entirely legendary, at others it was at least based on fact. Certain tales are repeated over and over again in children's history books: King Alfred and the cakes, or King Canute and the waves (a very popular incident in both England 8 and America, because of its moral and religious overtones). Then there were dramatic events like the loss of the White Ship, Captain Smith and Princess Pocahontas or Roland in the Pass of Roncevalles; also frequent re- 8 telling of the stories of great heroes like Frederick Barbarossa or Joan of Arc 6 and even mythical medieval heroes like Guy of Warwick, popular on both 8 sides of the Atlantic. History was a more positive subject than it can be today; the writer knew exactly where he (or more often she) stood and expressed his or her opinions strongly. On the whole all recent rulers received remarkably favourable and uncritical mention (perhaps this was all part of the nineteenth-century attitude to progress, in which 'latest' must mean also 'better'). It is against a conception of history very different from the one presented to children today that we shall now consider some of the non-text-book histories produced for the young.

Among the early English works on the study of history for the young was *A History of England in a Series of Letters From a Nobleman to His Son*. This work, published anonymously in 1764, was by Oliver Goldsmith, and though intended for youth of college age, it showed an appreciation of what constituted history which was too often sadly lacking in its successors:

... from history, in a great measure, every advantage that improves the gentleman, or confirms the patriot, can be hoped for; ...

Yet, still, nothing can be more useless than history, in the manner in which it is generally studied, where the memory is loaded with little more than dates, names, and events. Simply to repeat the transaction is thought sufficient for every purpose, and the youth, who is applauded for his readiness in this way, fancies himself a perfect historian. But the true use of history does not consist in being able to settle a genealogy, in knowing the events of an obscure reign, or the true epoch of a contested birth; this knowledge of facts hardly deserves the name of science: true wisdom consists in tracing effects from their causes. To understand history is to understand man, who is the subject. To study history is to weigh the motives, the opinions, the passions of mankind, in order to avoid a similitude of error in ourselves, or profit by the wisdom of their example. ... In short, not the history of kings, but of man, should be your principal concern, ...

History, in general, is precious or insignificant; not from the brilliancy of the events, the singularity of the adventures, or the

CAPTAIN SMITH

AND

PRINCESS POCAHONTAS;

AN INDIAN TALE.

PHILADELPHIA:

PRINTED BY THOMAS L. PLOWMAN, FOR THE
AUTHOR, AT HIS BOOK STORE, NO. 86,
ARCH-STREET, OPPOSITE THE
PRESBYTERIAN CHURCH.

1805.

Pocahontas ran with mournful distraction to the block

Guy earl of Warwick of great renown,
Whose storys told in every Town.
Through every Village as you go.
You'l hear of Guy & a monstrous Cow.

This Cow so mad none dare come near,
For all she met destroyed were.
Old or young, brisk, grave or gay.
Were tumbled or tossed if in her way.

Opposite top:
80 THE NEW CHAPTER OF KINGS; OR,
THE HISTORY OF ENGLAND IN
MINIATURE FOR THE USE OF CHILDREN.
C. Knight & Co, 1843. 17 × 12 cm.
In its 'rhyming couplet' approach to
each reign ('to be learnt by rote'),
this work looks back to its
eighteenth-century predecessor
(plate 79). Contrast the way in
which this event has been portrayed
by the unnamed artist, with the
highly finished picture produced
twenty years later (plate 81).

Opposite bottom:
81 THE PICTURE HISTORY OF ENGLAND
... ACCOMPANIED BY AN HISTORICAL
SUMMARY, SUITED TO THE CAPACITIES
OF YOUTH. Cassell, Petter & Galpin,
1861. (One of Cassell's family picture
books). 26 × 19 cm. A good example
of Victorian book illustration,
which may be compared with the
earlier and much cruder
representation of the same event
(plate 80).

Top left:
82 CAPTAIN SMITH AND PRINCESS
POCAHONTAS: AN INDIAN TALE by
John Davis. Philadelphia,
T. L. Plowman for the author, 1805.
A story featuring in both English and
American history, this type of
exciting adventure was popular
throughout much of the nineteenth
century.

Bottom left:
83 THE WONDERFUL EXPLOIT OF
GUY, EARL OF WARWICK.
Philadelphia, W. H. Morgan
[*c.* 1830]. This book is engraved
throughout and printed on one side
of the page only; the original
illustrations are hand-coloured.
Guy of Warwick was a folk hero
whose exploits were enjoyed on both
sides of the Atlantic.

greatness of the personages concerned, but from the skill, penetration, and judgment of the observer.

The wisdom contained in this passage was rarely taken to heart by subsequent writers for the young. Goldsmith was not greatly concerned here with the pointing of moral lessons, though they were of course implied. Other writers of the same period were less reticent. In the preface to *A New Roman History, From the Foundation of Rome to the End of the Commonwealth* published by F. Newbery in 1770, we read:

The principal advantage derived from the Study of History, is the Knowledge of men and things. We there see mankind rising suddenly to the highest pitch of glory and grandeur, and in an instant falling

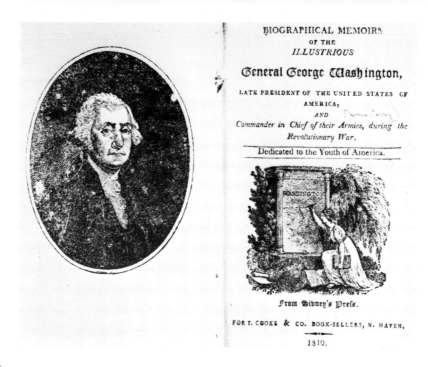

BIOGRAPHICAL MEMOIRS
OF THE
ILLUSTRIOUS

General George Washington,

LATE PRESIDENT OF THE UNITED STATES OF
AMERICA,
AND
Commander in Chief of their Armies, during the
Revolutionary War.

Dedicated to the Youth of America.

From Sidney's Press.

FOR I. COOKE & CO. BOOK-SELLERS, N. HAVEN,
1810.

Right:

84 BIOGRAPHICAL MEMOIRS OF THE ILLUSTRIOUS GENERAL GEORGE WASHINGTON, LATE PRESIDENT OF THE UNITED STATES OF AMERICA by John Corry. New Haven, I. Cooke & Co. 1810. 13.5 cm. An early illustrated edition of this work, specifically designed for 'the youth of America'.

Opposite top:

85 TRUE TALES OF OLDEN TIME, SELECTED FROM FROISSART by R. M. Evans. 2ed. W. Smith, 1842. 17 × 12 cm. An interesting attempt to match a medieval illustration to the text, reflecting the Gothic Revival of the period. Nevertheless, although influenced by contemporary manuscripts, the figures still look rather like Victorian gentlemen in fancy dress.

Opposite centre:

86 THE WARS OF THE JEWS, AS RELATED BY JOSEPHUS, WITH ADDITIONAL FACTS FROM JEWISH HISTORY. ADAPTED TO THE CAPACITIES OF YOUNG PERSONS. 4ed. John Harris, 1832. 17 × 11 cm. Like many of Harris's publications, this book is illustrated by engravings, placed two to a page. These have considerable brilliance of effect, and show an attempt at archaeological exactness mixed with romanticism that is reminiscent of the paintings of John Martin.

Opposite bottom:

87 A SERIES OF PRINTS OF ROMAN HISTORY DESIGNED AS ORNAMENTS FOR THOSE APPARTMENTS IN WHICH CHILDREN RECEIVE THE FIRST RUDIMENTS OF THEIR EDUCATION, by Sarah Trimmer. J. Marshall, 1789. 10 × 9 cm. A number of these small books of prints were issued to accompany separately printed texts. While trying to give an authentic 'period' picture, the result is nevertheless completely eighteenth century Neo-classical.

again into obscurity: we are there taught, that Virtue only is the true source of happiness; and that, however prosperous and triumphant vice and wickedness may be for a time, it will at last sink beneath the influence of truth and justice.

We may look upon History as the first master that children should have, equally fit to amuse and instruct them, to form their minds and hearts, and enrich their memories with an infinite number of facts as agreeable as useful. . . .

The chief end in the study of History is to dispel the false prejudices which reduce us, because they please us; to cure and set us free from the vulgar errors, which we have gradually imbibed from our infancy; to learn us to discern the true from the false, the good from the bad, and to distinguish between solid Greatness and vain Pride.

This was certainly very high-minded, but history does not provide a neat pattern of rewards to virtue and the punishment of vice. It is interesting to see that among those held up as a pattern 'for the improvement and entertainment of British youth' was Peter the Great: *The Father of His Country: or, the History of the Life and Glorious Exploits of Peter the Great, Czar of Muscovy* by W. H. Dilworth, was published in 1758. Also following in the steps of the great-man theme was Dodd's *The Beauties of History: or, Pictures of Virtue and Vice; Drawn From Examples of Men Eminent for Their Virtues, or Infamous for Their Vices. Selected for the Instruction and Entertainment of Youth.* Both these later works were illustrated (unlike Goldsmith's *Letters*), one with copper plates, the other with woodcuts. The importance placed on the study of great men of the past was not confined to Britain, as we can see from the example of *Teutonia* by E. Maukisch or the various biographies of George Washington. The idea that illustration added to the impact of the written text was fully appreciated in the history books. But there was a greater difficulty inherent in the illustration of history tales than in most children's books. Not even among adult publications was there an accurate awareness of period. How should one portray the ancient Romans or the medieval kings – or even the folk heroes? Imagination had full play here, with some surprising results.

The educated person of the eighteenth and nineteenth centuries would be well-versed in the classics and therefore the representation of these periods should have been well within the compass of the children's writers. Moreover, the late eighteenth century saw the beginning of the disinterment of Pompeii and Herculaneum, and the popularity of neo-classical art. On the whole, details in pictures of the Greeks and Romans showed a positive attempt to be historically accurate, and the *Series of Prints* chosen by Mrs Trimmer to accompany separately published texts were good examples of this attempt at accuracy. Nevertheless, the result was still surprisingly contemporary and, with all its 'Roman' details, the interior looks remarkably like that of a stately eighteenth-century home! (plate 87).

When it was a question of the illustration of English history, we can trace a great deal of change during the period from the mid-eighteenth to the mid-nineteenth century. The romantic approach to the Middle Ages which led to Horace Walpole's mock-medieval castle at Strawberry Hill and the subsequent influence of 'Strawberry-Hill gothick', found little echo in works for children. The simple illustrations of the earlier and lighter books contented themselves with portraits of kings and queens (mostly imaginary) and a few stylized actions. But the development of the scholarly attitude to the past, which we see in the representation of Biblical scenes, also appeared in the attempts at accurate 'period' flavour in the representation of historical scenes. Interest in the study of illuminated manuscripts, which was a feature of the mid-nineteenth century onwards, was reflected in the style of some of the pictures which appeared in children's books. Archaeological discoveries in the Middle East were beginning to impinge on the writing of those concerned with such works as the Josephus,

New-York

Pennsylvania

United States

published by Harris in 1824. *The Wars of the Jews* was illustrated with
wonderfully romantic steel engravings in which there were echoes of the
might that had been Babylon and Assyria.

The eighteenth century was less conscious of nationalism than the
nineteenth, which saw the rise of a number of nation states and the
unification of Italy and Germany. In France the Napoleonic legend was
consciously fostered by some sections of the population and made good
reading for all ages, but earlier events in French history were by no means
neglected in books for children. If the general trend of nineteenth-century
history writing inclined to the nationalistic, it is nevertheless noticeable that
in America much English history continued to be read by the young. This
was no doubt in part a result of the general pattern because English
books crossed the Atlantic during the first half of the nineteenth century
as at other periods. More surprisingly we find native productions of the same
sort, such as Blaisdell's *Stories from English History*, published in Boston in
1897. But of course America was very conscious of its own history, of
stirring events from the time of the Pilgrim Fathers to the Civil War. The
young had to be kept informed, as we can see from such works as *Young
Folks' History of the Civil War* by Clara E. Cheyney, published in Boston
in 1884.

Many writers for children claim that their books for home reading started
as stories told to real children. The work known as *Mrs Markham's History
of England*, written in fact by Elizabeth Penrose, opened thus: 'This little
work . . . was originally begun for the use of my own children'. The conversational method was employed, but as in so many books of its kind, the
'conversations' were extremely thin; even so, the author felt the need to
apologize for the lighter aspects of them: 'Many of the observations which I
have put into the mouths of the children, especially into that of the little girl,
may, I fear, be thought frivolous'. Being childless was no hindrance either
for one of the most famous works, written by Lady Callcott, was *Little
Arthur's History of England*, which begins: 'Though I have not the happiness
to be a mother . . .' and went on to state that it had been written for a real
little Arthur, and expressed the fear that it might not be 'amusing enough
to answer the purpose of those who wish children to learn everything in
play'.

On the whole one could rarely accuse the Victorians or their predecessors of being frivolous, especially where education was concerned.
Even those who took up original sources, such as Josephus, were anxious to
explain away the lighter (and more interesting) parts: 'Aunt Jane' said in
her preface, 'I hope, however, that this is an age when reading for
amusement alone is gone by' – had it even arrived in 1824? 'Uncle
Rupert' (R. M. Evans) in *True Tales of Olden Time, Selected from Froissart*
was even more concerned lest his lofty attempt to produce something
which deviated from strict historical relation might be considered too
entertaining:

AFTER THE BATTLE OF CRECY

FROM A WATER-COLOR BY H. S. MARKS, A.R.A.

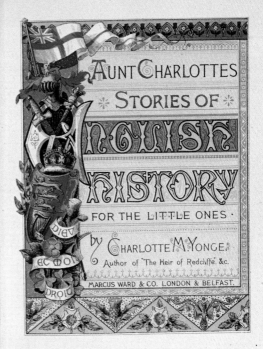

AUNT CHARLOTTE'S
STORIES OF
ENGLISH
HISTORY

FOR THE LITTLE ONES·

by CHARLOTTE M. YONGE,

Author of "The Heir of Redclyffe" &c.

DIEU
ET MON
DROIT

MARCUS WARD & CO. LONDON & BELFAST.

MARCUS WARD & CO.

KING ALFRED AND OTHERE.

Round in a fiery ring Went the great sun, O King.

Kronheim & Co.,
London.

Opposite:

91 PICTURES OF ENGLISH HISTORY: FROM THE DRUIDS TO MAGNA CHARTA. George Routledge & Sons [1868]. (New series of shilling toy books.) 26 × 22 cm. One of a set of four 'toy books' of English history published by Routledge and colour printed by Kronheim & Co.

Left:

92 PETITE BIBLIOTHÈQUE DES CHRONIQUES DE L'HISTOIRE DE FRANCE. . . . (Little Library of Chronicles of the History of France. . . .) par A. Mazure. 2ed. Paris, P. C. Lehuby (1842). 17 × 10 cm. A work in two volumes with a few engraved illustrations.

Below:

93 STORIES FROM ENGLISH HISTORY, FROM EARLIEST TIMES TO THE PRESENT DAY by Albert F. Blaisdell. Boston, Ginn & Co, 1897. This edition of Blaisdell's work 'for school and home use' indicates the continuing American interest in English history.

To supply the youthful mind with an additional stimulus to the study of history, by leading it to the well-head, and giving it to taste of the unpolluted waters of knowledge, has been the object of this little volume; . . .

To introduce our young readers to such an author; – to show them that history is not a mere dry catalogue of dates and of events; and thus to aid and encourage them in the pursuit of a study tending so especially to enlarge the mind and form the judgement, – has been our aim, which we trust will be found not altogether unsuccessful.

Nevertheless there were attempts at what one might call 'fictionalized' history, which offered a parallel to those strange, pseudo-historical tales so common in the late eighteenth century. Of these perhaps Sir Walter Scott's *Tales of a Grandfather* may be considered one of the best. But too often these could lead to the sort of style employed by Agnes Strickland, where on occasions her attempts at 'period' dialogue almost swamped the intrinsic charm of her stories. Here is an example from her *Tales and Stories from History*, 1836:

'What ho! Philip,' shouted Sir Ralph, 'hast thou turned fool, or art thou mad, to trust the noblest horse in Christendom to thy unlucky imp, Roger, who hath scarcely wit enough to be trusted with the shoeing of an ass?'

and again:

> 'Ah, thou naughty varlet,' said the knight, 'how is it that I find the heir of Fitz-Arthur practising the low craft of a farrier?'

Throughout the nineteenth century the study of history retained its high standing, though for many a young reader it must have seemed one of the more arduous studies. Most books were serious and packed full of facts, many of them were intended to be learned parrot fashion; even a book for quite young children could start off:

> People or nations are divided into *barbarous* or *civilized*. Barbarous nations are those who live a savage life; civilized nations are those who are skilled in arts and sciences.

Nevertheless, as the century progressed and there was greater general awareness of the sense of period, there was a softening of attitudes to the seriousness of history. Charles Dickens, in his *Child's History of England*, 1853–54, was one of the many popularizers, while the improvement in the standards of design and reproduction of book illustration made it possible to produce a work which could attract by both its content and its format. The introduction of colour printing must have increased the impact of these later books on the young reader. The old 'folk histories' continued to appear while, at the same time, there was a complete lack of interest in the social aspects of history. The modern child may not know the dates of his kings, queens and presidents but he probably has some idea of what life was like for, say, his medieval counterpart, which he has derived from reading, from illustrations, or from television. It must be remembered also that certain works of fiction, such as some stories by Sir Walter Scott, and, later by G. A. Henty, were set in an historical period, and many a child could absorb a sense of period better this way than in his formal history reading. Today we both know too much and are possessed of more doubts, so that the interpretation of history cannot be so positive as in the eighteenth and nineteenth century. Nevertheless, thanks largely to the quality of much historical writing and the power of television, history can be a far more vivid experience for the modern child than Little Arthur could have imagined.

8 Geography and Travel

Geography and travel were among the subjects which appealed most to the nineteenth-century educator, as compared with his eighteenth-century predecessor. There had, of course, been books in the late eighteenth century which endeavoured to give young minds some idea of the world around them, but nothing like the spate that poured forth in the nineteenth century. It was as if the curtain had gone up on the world scene, and children must share the view. To some extent foreign lands were brought nearer by increasing numbers of travellers abroad. For the British people this was especially true: English commerce was penetrating to the farthest parts of the earth – Lord Macartney's embassy to China had been sent in the year 1793 – the trial of Warren Hastings, which lasted from 1788 to 1795, had brought India very much to the forefront of people's minds, and participation in the long wars of the Napoleonic era had taken many Englishmen to various parts of Europe. Just before the end of this period had come the 1812 war with the United States, though there had of course (wars apart) been a long tradition of transatlantic journeying. The wars had, to some extent, prevented many people from travelling who might otherwise have done so; there could be no old-style Grand Tour during the upheavals on the continent. Once Napoleon was safely deposited on St Helena there was a rush to make up for the lost years. As the nineteenth century grew older there came the development of the railways which led to far greater mobility among all classes than had been possible before. In 1841 Thomas Cook arranged his first 'tour' in England, and in 1856, following his success in transporting the crowds to the Great Exhibition of 1851, Cook sent out the first of many tours to the continent. These nineteenth-century tourists were very different from the aristocrat making a leisurely Grand Tour, and their interests were likewise different.

All this excitement about the world around had to be passed on to the young, but there seems to have been little desire on the whole to do more than to take advantage of the parents' interest, without regard to standards or accuracy in text or illustration. In the majority of books on other lands intended for children's reading, the type of information conveyed was abysmal – the briefest and often most misleading statements were considered sufficient for the needs of the 'little tarry-at-home traveller'. This was the phrase frequently used in the titles of works by the Rev Isaac Taylor who, in the early nineteenth century, went round the continents (in book form), instructing the child and illustrating his text with a series of engraved plates. How did such writers find their illustrations? Very few could have been drawn by people who had actually seen the places thus depicted. In contrast to these rather spaciously produced works, by the middle of the century came the highly informative books of the 'Peter Parley' type. Crammed with information and usually characterized by a square format, they made great use of small woodcuts. But the illustrations were for the most part rather cramped in style and not very adequate for the depiction of exotic places; moreover the solidity of such fare must have

85

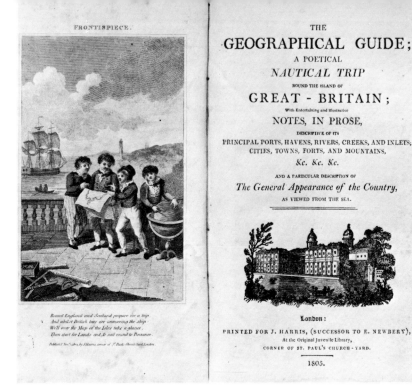

FRONTISPIECE.

Round England and Scotland prepare for a trip
And whilst British tars are answering the ship
We'll over the Map of the Isles take a glance,
Then start for Lands-end, & sail round to Penzance.

Published Nov.r 1804 by J.Harris, corner of S.t Paul's Church Yard, London.

THE
GEOGRAPHICAL GUIDE;
A POETICAL
NAUTICAL TRIP
ROUND THE ISLAND OF
GREAT - BRITAIN;
With Entertaining and Illustrative
NOTES, IN PROSE,
DESCRIPTIVE OF ITS
PRINCIPAL PORTS, HAVENS, RIVERS, CREEKS, AND INLETS;
CITIES, TOWNS, FORTS, AND MOUNTAINS,
&c. &c. &c.
AND A PARTICULAR DESCRIPTION OF
The General Appearance of the Country,
AS VIEWED FROM THE SEA.

London:
PRINTED FOR J. HARRIS, (SUCCESSOR TO E. NEWBERY),
At the Original Juvenile Library,
CORNER OF ST. PAUL'S CHURCH-YARD.

1805.

96 THE GEOGRAPHICAL GUIDE; A POETICAL NAUTICAL TRIP ROUND THE ISLAND OF GREAT-BRITAIN; WITH ENTERTAINING AND ILLUSTRATIVE NOTES, IN PROSE [etc.]. Printed for J. Harris (successor to E. Newbery), 1805. 17 × 10 cm. During the long continental wars which followed the outbreak of the French Revolution, the English became increasingly interested in their own country. The literature on the houses of the aristocracy was implemented by accounts of industrial England, watering-places and scenic beauty. Unfortunately, the illustrations to this book were poorly drawn and badly printed.

made the superficiality and inaccuracy of the 'picture-book' type seem eminently preferable to all but the most dedicated armchair traveller.

In contrast to the rather casual nature of much of the foreign travel material, many of the books on major cities like London, New York or Paris were usually of higher quality. This emphasized the authors' lack of personal knowledge – one might almost say personal study – of remoter places, even when writing a book on the subject. No doubt the information in many of the London books, for example, was taken from other printed sources and the plates frequently re-used. Nevertheless the books on famous cities were a far more lively collection. The method of presentation varied. Sometimes they were written on the 'question-and-answer' system, sometimes they took the form of letters to the family at home. For us these writings for children are of particular importance, revealing, in a detailed way that adult books do not, much of the contemporary urban social background, as well as offering information about long-vanished buildings and forgotten customs.

Although there were early attempts to supplement with more exotic fare the subjects it was normally expected a child should know, there is no doubt that on the whole, throughout much of Europe and America in the eighteenth century, it was believed to be a parent's main duty to pass on to his children his own views on religion, moral improvement and social behaviour.

In Britain, interest outside these subjects was centred for the most part on the British Isles and its capital. Indeed, following the outbreak of the French Revolution in 1789 and the virtual abolition of the Grand Tour, a whole generation of middle-class children were growing to maturity with little opportunity to set foot outside England or to meet many people who had recently done so. Meantime England's dependence on her overseas trade and her own industrial development was underlined by events. Curiosity about foreign places continued to exist, though in a modified form, during this period: *Captain Cook's Voyage to the Pacific Ocean* was one of the tiny illustrated books issued in the *Juvenile or Child's Library* by John Marshall in 1800. But rather more typical was *The Geographical Guide* which took a 'poetical nautical trip' round Britain in 1805. The illustrations in this work however were so crude as to be almost worthless, and gave little indication of what the same publisher, John Harris, was to achieve with his instructional books in another ten years or so. In 1815 the Battle of Waterloo opened up the continent again for English travellers, and there was renewed interest in seeing foreign lands. At the same time in many countries there was a great thirst for knowledge of all kinds about a world whose confines were being constantly enlarged, both physically and mentally. As Darton[1] has said of the United Kingdom, 'All the habitable globe was an open Aladdin's cave for the English-speaking fact collector'. In this atmosphere John Harris of London flourished. He excelled in the publication of different kinds of instructional books, usually well illustrated by engravings, and frequently hand-coloured. Many of the works discussed in the present book emanated from this publisher and his publications were among the most characteristic of the early nineteenth century. So successfully did Harris assess the requirements of his time that not only were his books popular in the United States, but works actually published in America also sometimes followed 'the Harris style'. He was fortunate that the writings of the Rev Isaac Taylor (1759–1829) and other members of the Taylor family exactly fitted his needs and that of the age. The series that began with *Scenes in Europe for the Amusement and Instruction of Little Tarry-at-Home Travellers* in 1818, for example, was to continue through a variety of different countries and to go into numerous editions.

Travel books for children in other countries on the whole appeared later. For curiosity about foreign countries to be aroused and fulfilled, reasonably settled political conditions were needed, and the continent of Europe took some time to compose itself after the upheaval of the Napoleonic Wars. Moreover certain countries such as Germany and Italy, still at this stage mere geographical expressions, consisted only of many small states. To some extent this was also true in the United States of America. Books to instruct the young about their own particular state, and about the larger country of which they were part, certainly were published, but in the early years of the nineteenth century large tracts of North America were empty, awaiting exploration and settlement. Many children were in fact doing the travelling which would be described to later generations of young people. By the time of the great trek west, much information on the land and its people would be incorporated not so much in dry, didactic texts, such as were common at the beginning of the century,

---

[1] *Children's books in England: five centuries of social life*, by F. J. H. Darton, 1958, p 219.

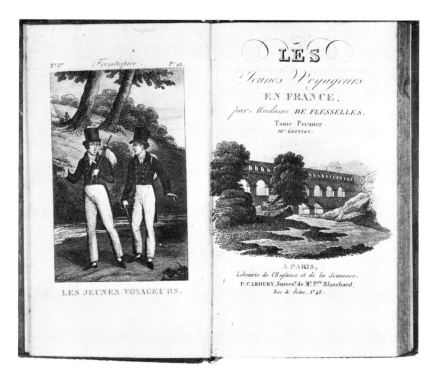

LES JEUNES VOYAGEURS.

97 LES JEUNES VOYAGEURS EN
FRANCE, HISTOIRE AMUSANTE,
DESTINÉE A L'INSTRUCTION DE LA
JEUNESSE, CONTENANT CE QUE LA
FRANCE PRESENTE DE PLUS CURIEUX
(The Young Travellers in France: an
Entertaining Story, Intended for the
Instruction of the Young, Containing
All the Most Interesting Things that
France has to Offer) par Mme de
Flesselles. 3ed. Paris, P. C. Lehuby,
1834. 14 × 8 cm. The engraved
frontispiece and additional title-page
to Volume I of this work. One of the
earliest travel books designed
especially for the young in France, it
can be compared to similar works
which were appearing in English-
speaking countries at the same time.

but in exciting adventure stories for boys. Not only young Americans
learned about their own history and geography in this way but, redressing
the transatlantic imbalance of the earlier period, many such tales found
avid readers in Europe.

An example of the old type of instructive book for children that was still
being produced even at the time when Harris was setting new, more lively
standards, was *The Elements of Geography*, published about 1820 in both 9
England and America. In this work the illustrations were hand-coloured
woodcuts, and each picture introduced children as extras rather than as an
integral part of the design. Nevertheless such a book did hint at wider
horizons. For the English publisher, after near-at-hand Europe, the next
place of greatest interest was the vast English-speaking area of North
America. In 1821 appeared *Scenes in America for . . . Little Tarry-at-Home* 1
Travellers, also by Isaac Taylor, and published in typical format by John
Harris. In some of the Harris books the illustrations, which being engravings
were usually printed separately from the text, were placed to face the text
to which they referred; in others (of which *America* was one), two pages of
illustration faced each other and the relevant text was on adjacent pages.
In the hand-coloured *Scenes in America* shown in plate 101, we can see both
the style of illustration and the blend of history and geography which the
plates contained. The text in such works was usually kept factual:

> The tobacco is planted in rows, kept very clear from weeds, and the
> lower leaves of the plant are pulled off, that only about a dozen or
> fifteen of the finest may grow. When these are fully ripe, they are
> stripped off, twisted together, packed in hogsheads, and sent to market.
> This is shred for smoking, and ground into fine dust for snuff.

or again:

AN ISTHMUS

Is a narrow neck of land between two seas or oceans: it connects a small tract of land with a larger, or one continent with another; as the Isthmus of Darian joins North and South America, and separates the Atlantic Ocean from the Pacific.

AN ARCHIPELAGO

Is a cluster of Islands; as the Archipelago between Turkey in Europe and Asia.

A PROMONTORY

Is a point of land stretching into the sea; and if it be considerably elevated, the end of it is called a Cape; as the Cape of Good Hope; a view of which I shall do myself the pleasure of presenting, in the good hope of giving you a more clear idea of a Promontory and Cape than you have hitherto had.

Carolina Rice.

The Rice plant has this peculiarity, that it grows best, where the ground is flooded with water. One large part of South Carolina is low marshy land, liable to be periodically overflown. The rice will always keep its head above water, even though this should rise to twelve or fifteen feet.

And so on throughout the book, with just an occasional intrusion of personal opinion. But this was not always the case. In his *Scenes in Asia*, for example, Taylor did not hesitate to express his disapproval of the various customs and manners of the countries with which he was dealing. He held up as a pattern the model of middle-class early-nineteenth-century Christian Britain, as seen by Isaac Taylor. In this he was not alone, for one of the most striking attitudes revealed in all British travel books written for children in this period, and even later, was the complacency with which all things British, Christian and nineteenth-century were regarded. Since much travel (and therefore information) was missionary-inspired, this perhaps was not so surprising in certain types of publication, and it certainly followed an earlier tradition established in the poems of Isaac Watts at the beginning of the eighteenth century:

> 'Tis to thy Sovereign Grace I owe,
> That I was born on British Ground,
> Where streams of Heavenly Mercy flow,
> And Words of sweet Salvation sound.'

Such patriotism was of course paralleled in other countries.

Another book which presented exciting episodes in North American history and geography was *Northern Regions: or A Relation of Uncle Richard's Voyages for the Discovery of A North-West Passage*, published by Harris in 1825.

Above left:

98 THE ELEMENTS OF GEOGRAPHY. A. K. Newman & Co. [*c.* 1820]. 17 × 10 cm. With the same format as *The Infant's Grammar* (plate 130), this work attempts to illustrate aspects of physical geography. The text is strictly didactic, and the introduction of children into the illustrations contributes little except that the publisher intended it for juvenile reading. An American version was published in Philadelphia about 1825.

Above:

99 ALL ABOARD FOR THE LAKES AND MOUNTAINS: A TRIP TO PICTURESQUE LOCALITIES IN THE UNITED STATES by Edward A. Rand. Chicago, Fairbanks & Palmer, 1885. The importance of railways in opening up America is reflected in this illustration, together with a growing desire to inform the young about their own country.

Above:

100 NORTHERN REGIONS; OR, A
RELATION OF UNCLE RICHARD'S
VOYAGES FOR THE DISCOVERY OF A
NORTH-WEST PASSAGE, AND AN
ACCOUNT OF THE OVERLAND JOURNIES
OF OTHER ENTERPRISING
TRAVELLERS. John Harris, 1825.
16 × 10 cm. The two incidents shown
here are: the Portage of the Drowned
and the escape of Captain Franklin
from a wounded buffalo.

Opposite:

101 SCENES IN AMERICA FOR THE
AMUSEMENT AND INSTRUCTION OF
LITTLE TARRY-AT-HOME TRAVELLERS
by the Rev. Isaac Taylor. Harris &
Son. 1821. 16 × 10 cm. One of a
number of *Tarry-at-Home Traveller*
books published by this prolific
author, some of which were issued
with the engravings hand-coloured.
Those shown here depict: emigrants
for conscience sake first landing in
America; Maryland proclaiming
liberty of conscience; Massachusetts
prohibiting the negro slave trade;
cultivating tobacco, Carolina rice;
and Rock Bridge, Virginia.

It consisted of a series of straightforward narratives, well-illustrated with engravings, somewhat reminiscent of boys' adventure stories of a later period. There were no captions to the plates and no direct references to them in the text; the explanation could only be found by diligently searching the neighbouring text. Nevertheless, the book was an attempt to present the various voyages of discovery to the far north of the continent in a form suitable for young readers and the illustrations, in spite of the shortcomings already mentioned, provided a vivid picture of the North American scene. This book, like some in the history section which were published in London and about North America, shows the interest in Britain concerning America, at a time when the predominantly English-biased publications there were being replaced by home-produced ones. From about 1830 onward we move into the 'Peter Parley' era. The original Peter Parley was Samuel Griswold Goodrich of New England, but his style so well suited contemporary taste in many countries that he had numerous imitators. Their identity has been carefully defined by Harvey Darton.[1] Exactly who was responsible for which publication is not so important here as the fact that the 'Parley' works were so much in accord with the spirit of the time as to be extremely popular, whether by the real or the fictitious author. 'Peter Parley' books were essentially factual, though they might be based on the ever-popular conversation or 'question-and-answer' method (some even had numbered questions at the end of the chapters). In this type, groups of children were gathered round a knowledgeable adult who, in return for a leading question, replied with a paragraph or more of solid information. Two typical examples are illustrated in plates 105 and 106, issued by different publishers and neither of them by the genuine Peter Parley. They indicate the widespread interest of the period in far-away places, the type of factual information conveyed, and the reasonable quality of the illustrations. Needless to say not all reached the standard of the two shown here.

At the same time that these informative volumes were being published, also on the market was a parallel series of books in the same field, those which followed the 'toy book' pattern. But although it would seem to us that the study of foreign countries would lend itself admirably to this sort of pictorial treatment, for the most part the publications by Dean or Darton, who specialized in early 'toy books', offered only the most stylized illustrations, and texts which it is quite alarming to think may have been taken seriously:

The Prussians are a warlike race,
Yet agriculture will embrace,
When peace forbids the sword and shield
They cultivate the harvest field.

[1] *Ibid*, p 229.

73

76

74

77

75

78

Published March 10 1821 by Harris & Son, corner of St Pauls.

Published March 10 1821 by Harris & Son, corner of St Pauls.

Baker.

See page 7.

Shipwright.

See page 73.

See page n.

See page 77.

Butcher.

London: William Darton, 58 Holborn Hill, 9 mo. 2nd 1824.

Lighterman.

London: William Darton, 58 Holborn Hill, 9 mo. 2nd 1824.

O Is Orion, that bright Constellation,
By which we steer true to our far destination.

P Point de Galle, we've left Aden behind,
But we hope, gentle reader, you will not much mind

Q Stands for Queer an epithet true,
Applied to the Natives here brought to your view.

This verse appeared below a crude cut of a town labelled 'Berlin', in a book called *The Young Traveller: or, a Brief Sketch of All Nations* published about 1850. An illustrated example of a rather higher standard than most was to be found in *The Overland Alphabet*, 1853, but even here an opportunity was missed, considering that the route illustrated was one travelled by many English people of the period. The quality lies in the freshness of the illustrations which are much more lively than the hack-work pictures of typical local figures in national costumes or vague representations of foreign towns.

But children's books shared in the general improvement in standards of book production which took place in the middle of the nineteenth century. Not only was there the advent of colour printing, but it had also become more common for well-known artists to acknowledge their work for the children's book market. An example of the better type of illustration was to be found in *Might Not Right: or, Stories of the Discovery and Conquest of America*, 1858. This book, which was written in the conversational fashion, had but few illustrations, but these occupied the whole page and were in the finished style of High Victorian book design; the name of the artist, Sir John Gilbert, appeared on the title-page. Likewise *The People of Europe*, published by the Society for Promoting Christian Knowledge in 1861–2, showed a genuine attempt at realism in its illustrations, even if the text sometimes fell below the truly informative:

> . . . [of] all the different people of Europe, none are so true to their friends, so gay and pleasant to live with, or so ready to oblige, as the kind-hearted French people.

PARLEY'S TALES

...ere is a large river in New Holland, called ...esbury. In this river there are swans, ... are quite black. All the swans of Europe, ...ica, and Asia are white, and it is very com... to say, ."as white as a swan." Such a ... as a black swan was not imagined to exist, ...ey were discovered in New Holland. ...ere is a very large bird found in this island ...l EMEU. This bird, also, may be seen at

What of the black swan?

98   TALES ABOUT CHINA.

The melons, one of which is seen cut, are water-melons; there are besides, grapes, white and red, figs, and peaches. This latter fruit the Chinese re-

Itinerant Fruiterer.

gard as the emblem of immortality. In the abode of Hien Gien, which is their Paradise, they imagine a peach tree, the fruit of which secures all those who eat of it from death.

Page 27.

107 MIGHT NOT RIGHT; OR, STORIES OF
THE DISCOVERY AND CONQUEST OF
AMERICA. Griffith & Farran, 1858.
15 × 12 cm. As transport improved,
the Atlantic crossing became less of
an ordeal, and the exchange of
visitors increased between the two
English-speaking areas of Great
Britain and North America. This
factual account of the American
story was illustrated by Sir John
Gilbert, who has managed to make
Columbus into a very 'Victorian
Gothic' figure.

The French have, generally, black hair and eyes, and dark complex-
ions. They are of a small race, as is particularly noticed when French
troops are compared with a regiment of English soldiers. The best-
looking among them are the people of Normandy, who are more
serious and thoughtful, and more fond of reading than the rest of the
French.

In France the country is more like Germany than England. Like the
former, a great part of it is divided into numbers of small farms
belonging to the peasants; half the people of France are occupied in
cultivating the land. The farms are not kept up neat and trim, as we
like to see them; the haystacks are half tumbling down, . . .

Having considered the wide-spread British interest in foreign lands,
particularly from about 1820 onwards, we will now look at the books
issued to inform English children about their own country. At a time when
manufacturing was so important it was a subject but little discussed in
books, especially for the young. The indefatigable Isaac Taylor and John
Harris had published *Scenes of British Wealth in Produce, Manufactures and
Commerce* in 1823. It showed various manufacturing processes, which were
perhaps more in line with the 'occupations' books than the travel books,
although the industries described were related to the different regions
taken in order. A similar but more important publication, again by Harris,
was entitled *The County Album*, 1829, which showed the features of each
county both topographically and industrially, in a series of hieroglyphics.
This method, which was best known for its use in the 'hieroglyphic Bible'
of the preceding century, lent itself quite well to geographical instruction.
But on the whole there was very little attempt to familiarize the young with
the topography of their own country, at least in out-of-school reading.

An exception to this was the interest shown in capital cities, particularly
London – even in America, where some children's books on that city were
also published. This was especially surprising considering that people
travelled relatively so little in the eighteenth and nineteenth centuries and
that provincial centres had therefore an importance which they have to some
extent since lost. But the capital of a country must always have possessed an
attraction as the seat of royalty or government, and as the goal for so many
aims and desires. Books on London for the young, for example, were many
and varied. A method of presentation might be to portray the city and its
sights through the letters sent by a young visitor to the family at home. Or
perhaps an imaginary family might themselves set out to study the city prior
to a visit. In this way a great deal of history, legend and topography was
poured into the interested child, and the subject received further stimula-
tion at the time of London's Great Exhibition of All Nations of 1851. Special
excursion trains and cheap days of admission brought into the capital at
this time many who would not otherwise have considered a visit (and also
encouraged many foreign visitors). Nor were publishers slow to note this

94

interest: *The Fine Crystal Palace the Prince Built, Little Henry's Holiday at the Great Exhibition, The House that Paxton Built* were some of the titles of books which took advantage of the tremendous interest aroused by the exhibition. Since the subject matter of the Great Exhibition was world-wide, it also stimulated people's interests in a great variety of hitherto unregarded topics.

Now, when the face of so many cities is changing rapidly, such works as the London books have a particular fascination, showing views and scenes of a city and a way of life which have long passed away. *The Public Buildings of London*, typical of many such picture books, showed, for example, a clear view of the front of Buckingham Palace very different from that of today. In such books the simple text often gave information of a basic kind which an adult guide book would ignore. What was then newest in town was described with pride, and certain buildings, such as the Royal Exchange (1824–5), appeared repeatedly in contemporary books on London. But such were the changes in books and views in a generation that anyone who remembered the works which had been published in his youth, and compared them with the ones he bought for his children, would immediately notice the difference in attitudes, book production and townscape.

A good example of a work which enjoyed long popularity in this field was *City Scenes: or, a Peep into London for Children*, first published in this form in 1806 and printed in an earlier version in Philadelphia in 1809. At the beginning of the book was a picture of a stage coach *en route* for London, faced by the introductory text:

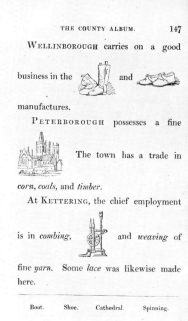

Above:
108 THE COUNTY ALBUM; CONTAINING FOUR HUNDRED TOPOGRAPHICAL HIEROGLYPHICS . . . FOR THE AMUSEMENT AND INSTRUCTION OF FIRESIDE TOURISTS. J. Harris, 1829. 17 × 11 cm. Following the method of the *Hieroglyphick Bible* (see plate 49), this work turns its attention to English topography. As usual in such books, the answers are prominently displayed at the foot of the page.

Left:
109 GRANDMAMA EASY'S ACCOUNT OF THE PUBLIC BUILDINGS OF LONDON. Dean & Co. [*c.* 1845]. 24 × 17 cm. Books on London for children took many forms; this is in the style of a 'toy book', and in the original the illustrations are hand-coloured.

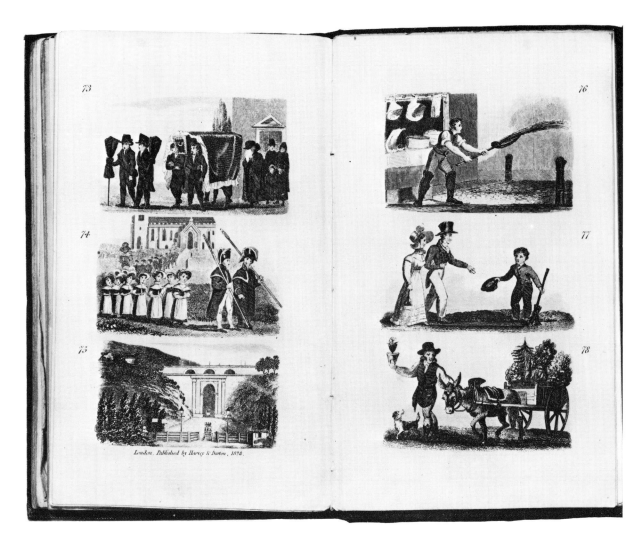

110 CITY SCENES; OR, A PEEP INTO LONDON FOR CHILDREN. Harvey & Darton. 1828. 17 × 11 cm. An extremely popular work by Jane and Ann Taylor, first issued in this version in 1806 but always published anonymously. The numbers on the plates refer to the paragraph descriptions of the scenes portrayed, which are entitled: the funeral, the charity children, Highgate tunnel, watering the streets, crossing sweeper, and the flower-pot man.

Here is Farmer Clodpole, who lives a hundred miles from London, coming to see it at last. They have just reached the top of a hill, and catch a fine view of the city.

'What! is that *Lunnun*, coachey? Well, I'm glad to see it at last; for I, that's only used to jog along a few miles in our cart, don't much fancy this jumbling and jolting. But what a smoke they are in, master coachman: I shall be glad enough to get back again, if I am always to be in such a *puther*. Pray, what's that there great round thing in the midst of the housen? Oh! St Paul's: why that beats our parish church all to pieces. Well, drive away, coachey, that I may see all the fine things; and nobody shall laugh at me any more, because I have not seen *Lunnun*.'

The book went through various editions, and the engravings were redrawn; by about 1845 the scene had to be radically altered. The new illustrations were full-page woodcuts, instead of groups of engravings as in the previous editions, and the revised opening paragraph was indicative of the new era:

Here is young Farmer Clodpole following the example of his good old father, in taking a journey to London to see the wondrous City Scenes of which he had heard so much. He has been persuaded by his little boy and girl to let them go also: they are quite a merry party, only the worst of it is that their mother, Mrs Clodpole, is obliged to stay behind to look after the farm. They have taken their places in a RAILWAY-CARRIAGE, and are flying away, as it seemed to them, from their little country village, beyond which the children had seldom been before. The four-horse stage-coach which took the old gentleman to town, has been given up for some years, in consequence of the famous railroad passing near the place; but this was the first time that ever the Clodpole family had ventured to travel by the new mode.

The illustration which faced this opening showed the Clodpole family on a railway platform.

Although redrawn on wood, many of the illustrations in the later edition were the same as in the earlier issues. But of course fashions had also changed in the intervening years, and in an illustration in the later edition, the crossing sweeper's customers were shown in mid-Victorian costume. Various improvements were commented on in the later work: new methods of paving the streets, of lighting them with gas, and even changes in methods of fire-fighting were mentioned. Such books abound in details that for us today provide interesting social comment, as well as reminding us of what we have gained and lost. In one of the illustrations to the earlier edition of *City Scenes* shown here, we see a picture of 'Watering the streets', whose accompanying text indicates one of the many aspects of daily life of the past which such books can so vividly bring before us:

London streets, in dry weather, are very dusty; this, when the wind blows briskly, annoys not only the eyes of those who walk, and of those who ride, but spoils the look of many a joint of meat. Pastry-cooks' and many other shops are much hurt by the dust; so that, at an early hour in the morning, many streets are watered by means of a scoop, and water pent up in the kennels, on each side of the carriageway.

In the same way the appearance of the crossing sweeper in both sets of illustrations reveals the importance of this long-vanished figure in the day-to-day life of the time:

Many of the crossings in London streets are often very dirty, and some little lads, who prefer doing even a dirty job to being idle, put down a board for the passengers to walk upon, which they sweep clean

CROSSING SWEEPER.
79

111 CITY SCENES; OR, A PEEP INTO LONDON FOR CHILDREN. Harvey & Darton [*c.* 1845?]. 13 × 11 cm. This work was often reprinted and eventually both text and pictures had to be revised; in this edition it has become a dumpy little book with wood engraved illustrations. This one shows the transformation of the crossing sweeper scene, which should be compared with no 77 in the 1828 edition (plate 110).

97

continually from mud or snow. They do not forget to hold their hats to those who make use of this convenience; and good-natured people seldom fail to drop a halfpenny into them, like the gentleman in the picture.

The travel book in all its forms, whether concerned with whole countries, regions, or individual towns, was one of the first to benefit from the introduction of photography as applied to book illustration. With this new method of making pictures, it was possible to show exactly selected aspects of various countries: their buildings, their landscape and their people. There was less and less excuse for representing the pyramids in unexpected juxtaposition, or showing St Paul's Cathedral in London as if it were set in an Italian piazza. With the ever-widening educational horizon, interest in books of this sort tended to flag as the century progressed and their study was more and more relegated to the classroom. By this time the child had won the battle to be allowed to read for pure enjoyment, and once this had been conceded, it was amazing how much instruction could be conveyed in a good story. The adventure story for boys, with its frequent emphasis on far-away places, however inaccurately portrayed, took the place to some extent of the equally inaccurate descriptions of the picture books, with their over-simplified labelling of countries and their inhabitants. In much the same way Scott, Stevenson or Henty, with their period tales, could offer similar courses in popular history. The travel book for children still survives and, though factual at times, is now very often based much more on the everyday life of a child in the country concerned, rather than on places or buildings. Moreover, the modern writer is not only better informed about his subject, but his child reader may be equally so. When the young think nothing of flying to the other side of the world for their school holidays you have to be very sure indeed of your facts!

9 Street Cries and Occupations

Nothing more surely brings us a picture of a lost world than books on the various street cries. When today we complain about the noise in the streets we forget that this was one of the complaints about city life most frequently made in the past; it is the method of making that noise which has changed so much. In the eighteenth and nineteenth centuries the street cry competed with the hubbub of traffic, especially in large towns, where itinerant traders were common. Also quite common were the children's books which tell us so much about them. On the whole, the content of these books of street cries was remarkably consistent. The traditional cry of the street vendor was given, then a little piece in verse or prose about him (or her), which might be either humorous or didactic, together with an illustration which either attempted verisimilitude or was merely meant to amuse. Whatever the motive, the result for us today is an interesting sidelight on then prevailing social conditions.

Even more valuable because they were nearly always serious publications, were books of trades or occupations. These explained to the young reader the means by which various commodities or services were brought to his use. Because they were meant to be informative about trade and manufacture, they provide detailed descriptions of tools, techniques and conditions of work. Such facts are not only of interest to the social historian but are also of great assistance to those people who are concerned with the artefacts of the past, whether in museums or elsewhere. For the most part, the descriptions of trades as they appeared in eighteenth- and nineteenth-century children's books were given as from the outside; to the child of the social class for whom these works were intended, on the whole, only the professions would be open. Today the same type of book can more fully enter into descriptions of contemporary trades and occupations, since not only may the writer speak from personal experience of his subject, but he can envisage that his young reader may also anticipate becoming involved.

THE GROCER.

My shop is well stock'd, neat, convenient, and
  handy;
Figs, almonds, and raisins, and sweet sugar candy;
Prunes, currants, moist sugar, and treacle, and spice,
Fine teas, barley sugar, and comfits, and rice.
With nice Spanish liquorice, when you've a cold;
And coffee and chocolate by me are sold.
If children are good, like good children I treat them,
And all my good things, O! how sweetly they eat
  them.

    A GROCER is a favourite with all classes
of people, young and old; his shop being
filled with the most delicious productions,
     B 2   from

Above:
112 JACK OF ALL TRADES. Harvey &
Darton. 1806. 15 × 9 cm. This work
is strictly didactic, apart from the
introductory verse at the beginning
of each section. The interior of this
early nineteenth-century shop
immediately impresses us with its
complete lack of advertisement or
display.

Left:
113 THE MOVING MARKET; OR, CRIES
OF LONDON FOR THE AMUSEMENT AND
INSTRUCTION OF GOOD CHILDREN.
Wellington, F. Houlston & Son
[*c.* 1820?]. 10 × 6 cm. One of several
chapbooks with this title and quite
striking in its simplicity; the
woodcuts are of an earlier date than
this particular publication.

24   25

Rabbits, O! a fine Rabbit.   Diddle, diddle, diddle Dumplings, O!
                         hot, hot, all hot.

Below:

114 THE JACK-OF-ALL-TRADES; OR, THE MERRY MERRY CRIES OF LONDON: IMPROV'D. Gainsborough [Mozley & Co., Lilliputian Book-Manufactory] 1794. 10 × 6 cm. One of the many chapbooks published in provincial centres, this contains a series of woodcuts, each with a poem and the particular 'cry' of the trade.

Opposite top left:

115 AUNT BUSY BEE'S NEW LONDON CRIES. Dean & Son [1852]. 24 × 17 cm. A typical hand-coloured wood-engraved 'toy book'. This is the title page; other smaller scenes have descriptive verses below the illustration.

Opposite top right:

116 THE SHILLING ALPHABET: TRADES OF LONDON. George Routledge & Sons [c. 1870?]. 26 × 22 cm. Colour printed by Leighton Brothers, this is a good example of the 'toy books' published by Routledge in great numbers. As in other books of its kind, the alphabet is merely used as a framework for the subject.

Opposite bottom:

117 THE BOOK OF SHOPS. VERSES BY E. V. LUCAS. ILLUSTRATED BY F. D. BEDFORD. Grant Richards [1899]. 23 × 31 cm. In this book, the interest is firmly centred on the illustrations and the descriptive text has little to add. The artist has signed his name clearly on the pictures, each of which is a work of art in its own right.

As might be expected from what has already been said in previous chapters, 'cries' and occupations books were more common in the nineteenth than in the eighteenth century. Nevertheless, the 'trade' books in particular have an especially honourable lineage, since they can be traced, in one form or another, back to the seventeenth-century *Orbis Sensualium Pictus* of the Czech writer Comenius (1592–1671) – the first true picture book for children. As has been said elsewhere (p. 114), Comenius was primarily concerned with the teaching of Latin, but he was among the first to appreciate the importance of illustrative matter in helping the child's memory. The coverage of subjects in *Orbis Sensualium Pictus* was almost as wide as life itself; first published in Nuremburg, it was early translated into a number of languages including English and frequently imitated. Among other aspects of life put before the young Latin scholar were the various trades and their implements – all of course with their Latin names since this was, after all, a Latin text book. But this illustrated compendium of occupations to be seen in street, shop or field, must have proved very attractive to the ever-inquisitive child and so, by the end of the

eighteenth century, we have the first of a long line of 'Jack-of-all-trades' books – a title frequently given to those volumes which set out to explain details of trades or occupations to the juvenile reader. A charming example was published in Vienna in 1789, with elegant engravings showing the

AUNT BUSY-BEE'S

NEW LONDON CRIES

LONDON: DEAN AND SON, THREADNEEDLE STREET.

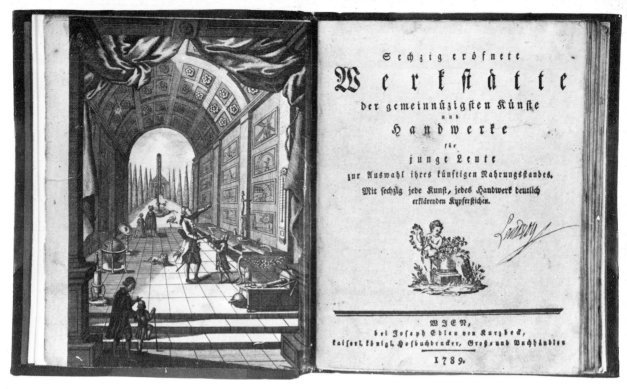

various trades in progress: this was *Sechzig Eröfnete Werkstätte der Gemein-nüzigsten Künste und Handwerke für die Junge Leute*. A similar type of work was that published in Paris in 1816, by M. Jauffret, *Petite École des Arts et Métiers . . . Ouvrage Destiné a l'Instruction de la Jeunesse*.

The long continental wars of the late eighteenth and early nineteenth centuries turned attention in the British Isles away from the wider prospects to the nearer, so that books of trades flourished, especially in the first two decades of the nineteenth century, when there was an increased awareness of commercial and industrial activity in England. The desire to instruct the young in such matters was strong and, for many a boy of scientific or inquiring mind, much of the material contained in these books must have seemed fascinating indeed, and may well have influenced his later career. For although most of the occupations described were those of the humbler workers, there was enough information to stimulate the enquiring child. Moreover, it was only from these books that he could normally hope to obtain any such knowledge; it was not at all the sort of thing he would be taught at school, where education was still firmly based on classical learning.

Most of these books had a didactic purpose, but it went often beyond mere instruction about a particular craft or occupation; the writers of the time were not prone to let slip an opportunity to make moral points as well. Certain themes constantly recur in these books; 'it was better to be busy than idle' could perhaps be proved from the content. But there was also a frequent suggestion that it was even fortunate to be poor, since poverty stimulated initiative in the young and encouraged them from their earliest youth to perform arduous and meritorious duties, and so prove a blessing to their parents! There was also a rather smug expression of gratitude (from well-fed warmth) for all the less agreeable tasks that provided the essentials of comfortable upper- and middle-class living. The

Opposite:
118 THE ZOOLOGICAL GARDENS: THE LION, TIGER, WHITE BEAR, WOLF, ORANG-OUTAN, BUFFALO. Frederick Warne & Co. [*c.* 1870]. (One of Aunt Louisa's London Toy Books.) 27 × 23 cm. In spite of its title, this 'toy book' has nothing to do with the zoo, except that the institution of zoological gardens in various countries enabled artists to study animals with greater accuracy. The illustrations, colour printed by Kronheim & Co., show the animals in their natural surroundings.

Above:
119 SECHZIG ERÖFNETE WERKSTÄTTE DER GEMEINNÜZIGSTEN KÜNSTE UND HANDWERKE FÜR JUNGE LEUTE (Sixty Workshops Revealed to Show the Useful Arts and Trades for Young People). Vienna, 1789. 20 × 17 cm. Shown here are the title-page and allegorical frontispiece. Other engraved illustrations depict the various occupations described in the text.

countryside too was seen through Arcadian spectacles – the milkmaid who had to rise so early in the coldest weather, whose hands were chapped and sore, was yet the possessor of a fine healthy complexion and all the better for her frugal life. The moral was hammered home on every possible occasion, though no doubt the young reader could as happily ignore it then as now.

Typical of the attitude to life and comfort it was thought necessary to imbue in young readers is the introductory chapter to *The Little Tradesman: or, a Peep into English Industry*, published by Darton in 1824:

Do you know, little Reader, that you are indebted to a great number of persons for the conveniences and comforts by which you are surrounded, and that various Manufactures and Arts are employed to provide you with food and clothing, and all the other necessaries of life?

The bread that you eat, – the clothes that you wear, – the house that you live in, – the book that you read, – and the paper you draw on, have employed hundreds of people in their composition and production, and a thousand inventions are constantly contributing to your various enjoyments. Ought not this reflection to awaken your curiosity? Should it not lead you to enquire into the nature of the objects around you, and induce you to endeavour to discover how it is that the ingenious hand of man contrives to turn the rough materials of Nature into articles of elegance and comfort?

Surely it ought! and the little book now presented to you will, I trust, produce the desired effect, and convince you that Industry and Art can perform wonders, tending not only to awaken our surprise and astonishment, but also to excite our gratitude to that great and good Being, who has abundantly provided for us all we can desire.

Today, these early books with their detailed instruction in methods of production, working conditions and other aspects of the artisan's life, provide a most fruitful source of social study, and one that has been largely left untouched. No detail was too small to pass on to the child and his complete ignorance was assumed in a way that it could not have been had the work been aimed at a more mature reader. Moreover, following the principles laid down in the previous century and much hallowed by use in the works of many eminent writers for children, any object, and indeed every object, could be used for this type of instruction. Maria Edgeworth's *Frank*, one of the series in *Early Lessons*, is perhaps among the best known of this type of book. Here is another typical attempt to make use of every opportunity that offered; it is to be found in Sara Coleridge's *Pretty Lessons in Verse for Good Children*, published in 1839:

120 PETITE ÉCOLE DES ARTS ET MÉTIERS (The Little School of Arts and Trades) by M. Jauffret. Paris, 1816. 13 × 8 cm. The popularity of juvenile instruction in trades and occupations was not confined to the English-speaking world; the French engravings shown here are similar in style to those produced by the London firm of John Harris.

Sweet China Oranges.

(PAVEMENT.)

St. Michael's oranges I vend,
   At one or two a penny,
Pray sir, how many may I send
   You home? "Why send—not any."

*Buy my Anchovies—Buy—my nice
   Anchovies.
Buy my Capers—Buy my nice Capers
   —Capers.*

How melodious the voice of this man,
   The capers he says are the best,
His anchovies too, beat 'em that can,
   Are constantly found in request.

121 THE CRIES OF YORK FOR THE AMUSEMENT OF YOUNG CHILDREN. York; J. Kendrew [1826?]. 10 × 6 cm. Compared with the *Moving Market* (plate 113), this chapbook shows a much greater attempt to depict a specific place. Kendrew of York was a prolific publisher of chapbooks.

THE PRUNE.

To give you this savoury Prune
   I'm sure was a very good turn;
My Herbert will eat it up soon –
   But first he has something to learn.

This dry wrinkled thing that you see
   Has once been a soft swelling plum;
It grew, like our plums, on a tree,
   And from a great distance has come.

The figs that are sold in the shop
   Were once like the firm shapely pear;
It always is better to stop,
   And find out what things really are.

Associated with the occupations or trades, but generally more light-hearted, were the 'cries'. These had been popular for a long time and were not originally children's fare. But it was quickly perceived that they too could be used didactically. They fell into two categories: those that really set out to instruct, and those that offered the information and let the child (or older reader) make of it what he wished. Some indeed are purely facetious, in typical mid-nineteenth-century style, using the itinerant tradesman and his traditional cries merely as a framework, in the way that the alphabet could also be used. Sometimes it is quite difficult to tell whether the books were aimed at the young or at the unsophisticated. This is particularly true of those which come in chapbook form, of which many survive, especially from the provincial printing centres. In some cases, as in the *Cries of York*, there was a definite attempt to locate the cries, and even to some extent in *The Cries of Philadelphia*, but for the most part the wandering trader and his characteristic call must have been recognizable

122 THE CRIES OF PHILADELPHIA.
Philadelphia, John Bouvier for
Johnson and Warner, 1810.
12 × 8 cm. Based on *The Cries of York*
(plate 121), this work is an indication
of the popularity of 'cries' books on
both sides of the Atlantic. And here
too, an attempt has been made to
appeal to local interest.

12

WATERMELONS.

"*Fine ripe Water Melons, Musk Melons, any Melons to day?*"

The melons brought to this market are from the state of New-Jersey, in which they grow in the greatest abundance.
They are considered, from their cooling qualities, to be very useful both to the sick and the healthy. They are sold so cheap, as to be within the reach of almost every person.

13

RADISHES.

"*Do you want to buy any Radishes?*"

These little girls are busy, in different times of the day, with a basket on their arms or heads, calling from door to door, to see who will buy; and it is not to be doubted, but that many, exclusive of the desire for the radishes, are induced to purchase, in order to encourage the little ones in their laudable examples of application and industry.—We are formed for labour; and it is not only an injunction laid upon, but an honour to us, to be found eating our bread by the sweat of our brows, and not spend our time to no profit.

in many parts of the country. It is interesting to see what items were sold in the street in those days – one did not go out and buy so much as wait for the goods to come to the door. This state of affairs persisted in some areas until the beginning of the present century, and it is only within comparatively recent years that the last of the surviving street cries has more or less ceased.

The familiarity of street cries to the young is brought out in a passage which occurs in *London Melodies* of 1812. In this, reference was made to the way in which children imitated the cries. Indeed the whole passage is worth quoting, since it illustrates yet again that even the simplest thing could be turned to good use by the determined educator:

It is not the intention of the Writer to introduce the CRIES OF LONDON as a novelty, most young people being already pretty well acquainted with them; but hitherto they seem to have been considered as a vehicle for prints and amusement, rather than a source of information.

The Writer presumes the two might be blended, and that, while the eye traced terms familiar to the ear, from daily observation, the mind might gather a portion of instruction; though, from so simple a source: accustomed as children are, and correctly as they may mimic the cries of 'Water Cresses', – 'Hot Cross Buns', and 'Earthen Ware', they are not aware, perhaps, of the toil endured by the gatherer of the first, the nature of the event which gave rise to the second, nor the length of time we have enjoyed the comfort and convenience of the latter. Yet surely it would be as easy to impress on their opening ideas the nature of things as their names. And it is not unnatural to suppose, the child who is pleased to remember the verse, will be proud to retain the information attached to it. General knowledge is not to be acquired at once; every step towards it is of consequence; and although the present ascent be trifling, the Writer trusts it has sufficient foundation to answer the purpose intended.

Unfortunately the high intent of the preface is not matched in this case by the illustrations that follow, which are very black and coarse woodcuts. But illustration was perhaps less important in books of cries than in those on trades; for in the former, the main information was given in the words of the cry itself, which always accompanied any other printed matter. That this was quite important, anyone who has ever heard a street cry will know. For not only were the words traditional, but also the tones in which they were called or sung. No doubt many a child only found out from one of these books exactly what the crier was saying, although it must always have been quite obvious what was being sold. The trades books, and the occupations described in them, must always have benefited from illustration, and indeed the artists frequently endeavoured to portray all the processes involved, from raw material to finished item, as clearly as possible: a fact which must have been particularly important when trying to explain unfamiliar occupations to a child.

A somewhat similar type of book which must have been very popular, in view of the variations of it which are to be found, was the one which purported to tell the 'life history' of a particular commodity: a loaf of bread, a scuttle of coal, a cup of tea and other similar objects. These little books, which featured illustration rather than text, were of a sort that, brought up to date, could be enjoyed by the enquiring child today, since they were not heavily didactic but offer their information in an attractive way, frequently in verse form. Such works were obviously only meant to

123 THE HISTORY OF A SCUTTLE OF COALS IN RHYMES [by W. Newman] AND PICTURES [by W. J. Linton]. Griffith & Farran [1860]. 13 × 18 cm. One of a series of 'histories' (of tea, sugar etc.) in which the various processes of manufacture were illustrated and described in verse. This illustration is of the hand-coloured title-page designed by W. J. Linton.

GRIFFITH AND FARRAN, Successors to Newbery and Harris, Corner of St. Paul's Churchyard.

124 RURAL SCENES; OR, A PEEP INTO THE COUNTRY FOR GOOD CHILDREN. Darton & Harvey. 1806. 15 × 9 cm. The engraved plates, separated from the text to which they apply, give an entertaining and informative portrait of contemporary rural life, whereas the text tends to draw an idyllic picture, often contrasting simple country virtues with the moral laxity of sophisticated urban life. The work, by Jane and Ann Taylor, was published anonymously.

offer superficial information in a pleasurable way. This was, no doubt, also the intent of books like *The Cries of New York*, 1820, or *Aunt Busy Bee's New London Cries*, published by Dean and Son in 1852. But far too few writers for children could accept such a limited aim; they must go further and emphasize the lesson clearly for the young mind. In *Rural Scenes; or, a Peep into the Country for Good Children*, 1806, the authors constantly link the pictures and the text with more serious matters:

> Pretty innocent sheep, no more sporting for you upon the soft grass, and jumping about in the fresh air of a summer's day! You little thought, while you were so frolicksome, running and frisking among the daisies and butterflowers, what it would all come to! It puts me in mind of those thoughtless people, who do nothing but laugh and play, all their lives long, and forget how very soon they must die.
>
> When an innocent sheep is condemn'd to the knife,
>   It never can suffer again;
> But when a *man* dies, he must live a new life,
>   Forever, in pleasure or pain.

and again:

HAYMAKERS.

Here are two pictures of merry haymakers, as cheerful as the little birds that sing over their heads. Those at the top are mowing the grass down with sharp scythes, and the others are spreading it about with their pitchforks to dry. As soon as the sun peeps over the hills, in the morning, they come out, and begin their work; for a hay-maker would be ashamed to lie snoring in bed of a morning, when the sun is up, and the birds are up, and the sheep, and the cows, and the poultry are up; and the little insects are up, buzzing about in the heat of the sun; and every body is up who is not a sleepy, idle person.

The Little Tradesman; or, a Peep into English Industry, 1824, which was a later publication, had much more genuine information about the various occupations depicted. The section on the baker, for example, took up four pages of text, and described every stage from ploughing to baking in great detail; similarly explained were the occupations of the shipwright, the lighterman, the butcher and others. But here too the author could not leave the text to speak for itself: the section on the baker ended thus:

Yes, it is, I assure you, very laborious work to make bread; and I think all little boys and girls who are able to procure it, ought to be very grateful to the useful baker, as well as to the miller, and the

Ein Kutscher werd' ich, bin ich groß,
Dann peitsch' ich auf die Pferde los
Und jage über Stock und Stein;
Das wird ein prächt'ges Leben sein.
So denkst du jetzt, doch wachse erst,
Vielleicht, daß du's dann nicht begehrst.

125 WAS WILLST DU WERDEN? (What Do You Want To Be?) 2ed. Berlin, Weidmannschen Buchhandlung [1864?]. 26 × 20 cm. In this book, the detailed wood engravings by the artist Oscar Pletsch are the main interest, the verse being merely an accompaniment.[1] Each scene incorporates children, either watching or participating in the action depicted.

[1] A coachman's what I want to be, when I'm grown up,
Then I will whip up the horses
And chase over sticks and stones;
That will be a marvellous life.
That's what you think now, but grow up first
Perhaps then you will no longer want the same!

farmer, and the thrasher, and the little whistling ploughboy: – but, above all, they ought to reflect upon the goodness of Providence, who causes the wheat when it is sown in the ground to spring up, and who, in thus providing the food of thousands of families, gives employment to so great a number of our fellow-creatures.

The representation of trades and occupations was always good illustrative material in itself and, as it gradually became possible for children's books to be published free of all didactic intent, we find some very attractive examples of this type of book. *Was Willst du Werden?* is really just a picture book illustrated by the well-known artist, Oscar Pletsch; the accompanying rhyming text is unimportant. Routledge's 'toy books', so popular in the second half of the nineteenth century, rarely attempted anything more than very general instruction, if even that. *The Shilling Alphabet: Trades of London*, which, printed in colour by Leighton, was published as a 'toy book' in 1869, was certainly not designed to teach the alphabet since the accompanying rhymes would have been too difficult for a learner. It was simply a picture book showing various tradesmen at work, and intended to give pleasure rather than instruct. At the very end of the century we find *The Book of Shops*, where each illustration was a picture in itself; it was the artist's work which was important. *The Book of Shops* forms a fitting conclusion to this chapter since, by the date of its publication in 1899, buying and selling had moved away from the streets and the itinerant vendor and into shops; at the same time the old trades, unchanged for centuries, had already or were about to experience a fundamental transmutation which would mean that the processes and people delineated in the texts and illustrations of the children's books discussed in this chapter would become a part of social history.

Opposite top:
126 UNE FAMILLE DE ROUGES-GORGES (A Family of Robins) [by Mrs Trimmer]. Strasbourg, 1847.
15 × 10 cm. Mrs Trimmer's book, first published in 1786 with the title *Fabulous Histories*, went into many editions and was translated into several languages.

Opposite bottom:
127 ENTOMOLOGY IN SPORT, by two lovers of the science (the Honourable Mrs W. and Lady M.) TO WHICH IS ADDED, ENTOMOLOGY IN EARNEST. Paul Jerrard & Son [1859].
18 × 14 cm. The first part of the book consists of descriptions in verse, accompanied by hand-coloured illustrations of the insects described. The second, 'earnest' part is in dialogue form. The title-page and frontispiece shown here are hand-coloured lithographs.

UNE FAMILLE
DE
ROUGES-GORGES.

STRASBOURG,

Chez Vᵉ LEVRAULT, rue des Juifs, 33.

1847.

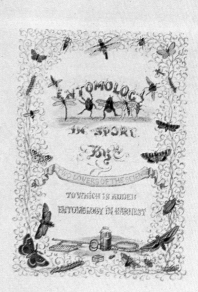

ENTOMOLOGY
IN SPORT

THE LOVERS OF THE SCIENCE

TO WHICH IS ADDED

ENTOMOLOGY IN EARNEST

TULIPE

A COLON, marked thus :

The colon consists of two dots, as you see;
And remains within sight whilst you count one, two, three:
Tis us'd where the sense is complete, tho but part
Of the sentence you're reading, or learning by heart.
As 'Gold is deceitful: it bribes to destroy'.
'Young James is admired: he's a very good boy:'

THE PRONOUNS.

At this moment a bustle was heard at the door
From a party of PRONOUNS, who came by the score.
And what do you think? Why I vow and declare
THEY would pass for the Nouns who already were there.
And THEIR boldness was such, as I live IT is true,
ONE declar'd HE was I, and one call'd himself YOU.
THIS, THAT, and the OTHER, they claim'd as THEIR own,
But WHO THEY are really, will shortly be known.

CONJUNCTIONS
join the words
together,
As,
men 'and' women,
wind 'or' weather.

10 Natural History and Science

Natural history, in its widest application, was among the most popular of all the subjects considered in this book for a number of reasons. In the first instance most people in the eighteenth and nineteenth centuries lived in rural communities – certainly this was true of Britain in the eighteenth century. Those who lived in towns were never far away from the country-side, even if their homes were in big cities like London, when Kensington was a village and Hampstead the haunt of highwaymen. Moreover, unlike their continental counterparts, the English aristocracy (and the upper-middle class who followed their lead) did not absent themselves from their estates to lead an exclusively town life around the court. The social season saw them in London (or Bath or Harrogate), but the hunting season saw them out of town; to be in town during the wrong period was to be quite out of fashion. On establishing his fortune the *nouveau riche* would immediately purchase a country estate and play the squire. So that most of the children with whom we are concerned in this book would have spent much time in country surroundings, and natural phenomena would be almost as familiar to them as household objects. Continental natural history books for children are on the whole rather less common, and in part at least this was probably due to differences in the social pattern.

Another important reason for the prevalence of books dealing with 'the brute creation' was the preoccupation of many writers, especially English-speaking ones, with religious and moral matters:

> God made all things. What we call the works of Nature are the works of God. It is our duty to study them, since the more we know of them, the more we perceive the wisdom and goodness of their Great Creator; who formed them to suit the modes of life for which they were destined, and bestowed upon them all the comforts of which their nature is capable.

So says the anonymous author of *Footsteps to the Natural History of Birds and Beasts*, a work published in both London and Philadelphia in 1803 and re-published a number of times in London, Baltimore and New Haven. It was no coincidence that so many clergymen were numbered among those who wrote about natural history, either for the young or for adults.[1]

It was one thing to study the birds and flowers – animals were not quite so popular at first – but foreign creatures – well, that was another matter. Nevertheless, the study of foreign as well as indigenous animals could not be ignored for they, even more than native ones, proved the truth of the philosophy all the natural history writers for children were anxious to propound:

> Natural History has always appeared to me a particularly suitable study for young people; as it excites the youthful mind to the con-

[1] The well-known work by the Rev Gilbert White, *The Natural History of Selborne*, was published in 1789.

Above:
132 BILLY LOVEGOOD'S HISTORY OF
BIRDS AND BEASTS: WITH
INSTRUCTIVE POEMS UPON EACH.
Recommended to be read by all
little masters and misses, who wish
to be acquainted with the natural
history of the animal creation.
R. Bassam [1795?]. 10 × 6 cm.
Illustrated with woodcuts, this work
shows how crude many cheaper
books for children often were: this
cost 2d. The compiler has not
neglected to draw a moral from each
creature depicted in the book.

Right:
133 HISTORY OF BRITISH BIRDS. The
figures engraven on wood by
T. Bewick. Vol. I: containing the
history and description of land birds.
Newcastle, by Sol. Hodgson for
Beilby & Bewick, 1797. 25 × 16 cm.
The high quality of Bewick's wood
engravings set a new standard for
illustration. His description of
birds and animals was as accurate as
his drawings of them.

templation of the infinite wisdom which has been shown in making all creatures form one vast whole; every part of which is in some way connected with, and dependent on, the rest. Nothing has been made in vain. Earth, air, and sea, are all peopled with living things, suited to the different situations in which they are to exist, and to the functions which they are destined to fulfil. The mole, for example, was intended to live under ground; and how wisely and how wonderfully it is suited for this purpose!

writes Mrs Loudon in *The Young Naturalist's Journey*, 1840. And so, during the whole period studied in this book, works on flowers, animals, birds, trees, insects – even shells – appeared in great numbers, aimed at various age groups and produced with varying degrees of accuracy.

Between the eighteenth- and nineteenth-century attitudes to the subject there were noticeable differences. As in all other spheres we have considered in this book, the truly technical work in natural history was more a feature of the nineteenth than the eighteenth century. On the whole, specialization does not appear to have been considered necessary, especially among the early writers – the same writer could produce a book on birds one day and something on the countries of Europe the next, while amateur writers on the subject proliferated. In a work where observation was of primary importance, any sharp-eyed child could prove the error of the writer; the safest course for the non-specialist was to compile rather than to compose. Compilation was at all times common among writers of children's books, but especially so among the natural history writers – with or without the permission of the original author or illustrator, or even a sideways acknowledgment. For this reason, the same illustrations occasionally recur in different works – perhaps reduced in size or reversed in the printing, but still recognizable from their original source. Bewick's work was particularly 'borrowed' in this way; where the cuts were not by him, they were frequently claimed to be 'after' him – sometimes a long way after indeed! But in borrowing Bewick's illustrations or descriptions, the writer was at least reproducing the work of someone whose reliability could

be depended upon. Many often-repeated illustrations came from less trustworthy sources so that, when the publisher reproduced pictures of the more exotic creatures, such as camel, elephant and rhinoceros (or unicorn!), the same strange figures appear again and again.

We tend to forget, because we have the opportunity of visiting zoological gardens and wild-life parks, that many a writer of the eighteenth and early nineteenth century never saw the animals or other creatures he was describing. The need for accuracy is never questioned now, when even quite young children are familiar with the basic features, of, say, an elephant or a lion. But looking at many of the illustrations in this chapter, the low standard of pictorial representation is often obvious. Anatomically correct drawing became more common as it became easier to study originals, so that hack work was less and less acceptable. In England the opening of the Zoological Gardens in Regents Park, London, in 1828 enabled a better knowledge of wild creatures to be obtained than had been possible when information could only be gained from such creatures as were currently on display at the Tower, or Royal Exchange. On the continent collections of animals had been started earlier – at Schönbrunn, Vienna, as early as 1752 – while the Jardin des Plantes in Paris was opened in 1793. But the popular zoos for the entertainment of the public coincided with increased general interest in natural history which was more typical of the nineteenth century. Greater accuracy in the description and delineation of natural phenomena of all sorts was now possible, partly because people were more interested. The natural sciences took their share in the passion for information which existed in other fields in the nineteenth century, and facts were duly passed on to the young in a series of instructive manuals, often of a very detailed kind. Mostly published later in the nineteenth century, they still tended to follow the conversational pattern laid down for such works in the eighteenth century. In these often quite technical works, the child's interjections did no more than provide the cue for a further monologue:

'I fear,' said Charles, 'that this new division will be rather difficult, for my father tells me that we must pay particular attention to the *hinges* of bivalve shells.'

'Then *apply* yourself to the study of hinges, Charles, and your difficulties will chiefly disappear,' answered Mr Elliot.

'The hinge of *Mya*, the first on the list, is easily known. The generic characters are, shell gaping at one end, hinge mostly with one thick spreading tooth, not inserted into the opposite valve. The *Mya* race burrow in the sand. Here is *Mya arenaria*, a large thick shell, frequent on the shores of Kent: . . .'

and so on for pages in *The Rudiments of Conchology*, 1837; but it could be paralleled by quotations from similar books on birds or botany. Nevertheless, such works were usually accompanied by very detailed illustrations

98   *The Natural History*

more fatal to their owners than the enemy. They formerly used to place a sort of tower on their backs, which held about six fighting men, who threw darts at the enemy.

The RHINOCEROS or UNICORN.

THE Rhinoceros is sometimes called the Unicorn, from his having one horn only, growing

134 THE NATURAL HISTORY OF FOUR FOOTED BEASTS, by Tommy Trip. Glasgow, J. & M. Robertson, 1802. 10 × 6 cm. Illustrated with woodcuts, this little book has a straightforward text, without any obvious moral message. An edition was published in New York in 1795.

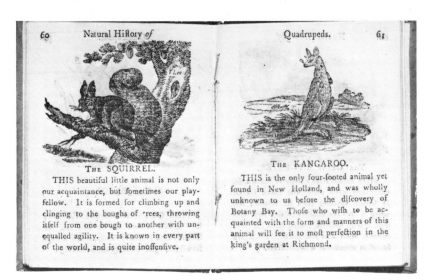

THE SQUIRREL.

THIS beautiful little animal is not only our acquaintance, but sometimes our play-fellow. It is formed for climbing up and clinging to the boughs of trees, throwing itself from one bough to another with un-equalled agility. It is known in every part of the world, and is quite inoffensive.

THE KANGAROO.

THIS is the only four-footed animal yet found in New Holland, and was wholly unknown to us before the discovery of Botany Bay. Those who wish to be ac-quainted with the form and manners of this animal will see it to most perfection in the king's garden at Richmond.

135 A CONCISE ABRIDGEMENT OF NATURAL HISTORY, IN FIVE VOLUMES. J. Marshall (1800). 9 × 7 cm. *Volume I: Quadrupeds*, of the set published in the *Juvenile, or Child's Library*. Some attempt has been made here to depict the creatures in their natural habitat, although the drawing of the animals themselves shows a need for greater accuracy. The text of 'The Kangaroo' reminds us how recently the frontiers of the known world had been pushed back.

which must have given the interested child all the information he wanted, unlike the very general books which were also on the market, or those which merely offered 'pretty stories' about various animals, especially when they came in such forms as *Pretty Stories About the Camel*, published by Dean and Co, *c.* 1845.

Although there was an increasing desire to give accurate information to the young, writers never lost sight of the Creator of all natural phenomena, even when the developments of science towards the end of the nineteenth century made it rather more difficult to express His part in the scheme of things in the words common to earlier centuries. *A Concise Abridgement of Natural History, in Five Volumes*, published by John Marshall for the Juvenile Library in 1800, put the contemporary point of view clearly:

> The engaging subject of Natural History presented in the form we have given it, and embellished with such a variety of engravings, cannot, we think, fail of proving acceptable to the youthful reader, particularly when it is considered as being, of all other studies, the most necessary to a polite and well-finished education.
>
> It softens the mind imperceptibly, leading us to this sublime truth, – That nothing is created in vain. This science is the only means by which we may know ourselves; by the attainment of which we learn to be grateful to the Supreme Being, for having created for our use, support, and protection, such a number of creatures.

The five little volumes with their engraved illustrations of all aspects of the natural scene must have been a great joy to the observant child, accompanied as they were by simple explanatory texts. By the time this was published, there had been available for over a decade one of the great classics of English writing on natural history, and one whose influence has continued in an uninterrupted line to our own day. This was uncompro-misingly (and misleadingly) entitled *Fabulous Histories; Designed for the Instruction of Children, Respecting their Treatment of Animals*, and was published by Mrs Trimmer in 1786. Her intention was set out in the 'Advertisement':

> It certainly comes within the compass of *Christian Benevolence*, to shew compassion to the *Animal Creation*; and a good mind naturally inclines

to do so. But as, through an erroneous education, or bad example, many children contract habits of *tormenting* inferior creatures, before they are conscious of giving them pain; or fall into the contrary fault of *immoderate tenderness* to them; it is hoped, that an attempt to point out the line of conduct, which ought to regulate the actions of *human* beings, towards those, over whom the SUPREME GOVERNOR hath given the dominion, will not be thought a useless undertaking: and that the mode of conveying instruction on this subject, which the Author of the following sheets has adopted, will engage the attention of young minds, and prove instrumental to the happiness of many an innocent animal.

26 This work was later known as *The History of the Robins*, and as such remained popular all through the nineteenth century. It was also translated into French. The story concerned a nest of robins, whose father and mother partook of the sentiments and affections of good parents, and the little fledglings behaved like human children. To imbue animals or birds with human personalities is an idea so common to us, that it is hard to appreciate the impact such a work made when it first appeared. Although the moralizing aspect was never forgotten, the story was told in such a way as to hold the interest of the young, especially when it concerned birds so delightfully named as Robin, Dicky, Flapsy and Pecksy. Nevertheless, as in the case of other fables, the anxious author pointed out that these stories were not true; they were merely intended to convey:

> moral instruction applicable to themselves, at the same time that they excite compassion and tenderness for those interesting and delightful creatures, on which such wanton cruelties are frequently inflicted, and recommend *universal Benevolence*.

Mrs Trimmer's tale of birds whose speech could be rendered intelligible to the young reader led easily to the next step, in which a particular bird or animal told its own tale – another *genre* which was to have continuous popularity. So we have works like *Memoirs of Dick, the Little Pony, Intended for the Instruction and Amusement of Little Masters and Misses*, 1816 – surely the ancestor of that other, late-nineteenth-century, nursery favourite *Black Beauty* – as well as many similar works which use the same method. Obviously this method was one which could best be used with animate objects, and birds, like animals, were particularly suited for this treatment. The text could be strictly didactic, or it could give its information in a more playful way, as in the following extract from *Birds and Insects; Dialogue in Prose and Verse Illustrative of Their Habits and Instincts*, written and illustrated by Jane Bragg, 1844:

THE SWALLOW-TAILED KITE.
'I am indeed a fine bird, as you say, my dear little Miss, but I am not proud, though I look as if I was. I am extremely graceful, I know, though I say it, that should not, perhaps.'

136 THE LITTLE BOTANIST; OR, STEPS TO THE ATTAINMENT OF BOTANICAL KNOWLEDGE by Caroline Halstead. Illustrations drawn and engraved by J. D. Sowerby, from sketches by the authoress. Part I. John Harris, 1835. 13 × 10 cm. This work, one of the volumes in *The Little Library*, shows the amount of detailed instruction which was available to children. The text is written in the conversational style so frequently favoured in the didactic books of the period.

CHAPTER V.

FIRST CLASS, MONAN'DRIA — EX.. JOINTED GLASSWORT. — SECOND CLASS, DIAN'DRIA — EX.: GERMANDER SPEEDWELL.— THIRD CLASS, TRIAN'DRIA — EX.: IRIS — GRASSES — THEIR SEVERAL PROPERTIES AND USES.

L. I FEAR, dear mamma, you will think me very stupid—I am quite vexed with myself; but I do assure you that I examined a multitude of flowers during your absence yesterday, yet not one could I find that contained a single stamen only.

M. I knew full well it would be the case, my dear Louisa; but I also knew, that unless you ascertained that fact from your own observation, you would not be satisfied with my saying so, or with being obliged to receive a

'Well, Mr Kite, I do think you are *rather* conceited after all; but this you ought not to be, for the same power who kindly bestowed on you all your perfections, could also in a moment rob you of every feather.'

Jane Bragg's work was based on reasonably sound observation but too often the poetical flights on the subject of natural history could deteriorate into bad verse. Not even the illustrations by Birket Foster could redeem the following, from *Birds, Bees and Blossoms*, by Thomas Miller, 1858:

I think of these things while I look on the ground,
Think the time will soon come when there will not be found
A bittern alive if you search England round.
For I know I am nearly the last of my race,
And that few will be found to fill up my place,
And that soon there will be neither vestige nor trace
Of the bitterns that boomed through long thousands of years.
Do please lend me something to dry up my tears.

and again:

SWALLOWS

Over city, and village, and spire,
Over streets that look like streaks of fire,
With all their blazing lines of gas;
Over vast pathless swamps we pass.

For the most part the works considered so far have been intent on something beyond the actual descriptions of the natural world. They were designed to point morals, give religious instruction, or indicate correct social behaviour, including humanity to both man and beast. If sometimes the lesson drawn appeared rather forced and the natural history suffered thereby, the author might still feel that his main point had been made, as in the anonymous book *The Beauties of Natural History*, published in Bath in 1777(?), where we find the following verse quoted from an earlier work by Cotton:

My Cow rewards me all she can,
(Brutes leave ingratitude to man;)
She, daily thankful to her lord,
Crowns with nectarious sweets my board.

But many writers, especially as the nineteenth century progressed, felt that
the study of natural sciences could offer something more:

The minds of the young are ever active; they will be employed about
what is good or evil. One object, then, in a rational scheme of education, must ever be, to provide engagements which will tend to their
improvement. And he who would be successful in this great work,
must render his lessons attractive and delightful. The works of God will
afford him an inexhaustible treasury for his aid. Parents and tutors
should be on their watch to find for their dear charge, sources of
legitimate pleasure; or they will seek for gratification in forbidden and
injurious paths; and especially, which cannot be too much guarded
against, in the company of the profane and dissipated. The pages of
this volume, the Author hopes, will show them, at least in some small
degree, how he would wish them to open to the delighted eyes of the
young, the ever-blooming, and ever-instructive leaves of the volume
of creation. He is assured, that the scenes it describes, with a very little
pains, may be carried out into action, since the book is only a transcript
of what has constantly taken place in his own family. He is indeed
greatly mistaken, if the habit of using the eyes and the understanding,
in the way he has recommended, will not be a perpetual source of
gratification and instruction.

This quotation, which we find in the preface to *The Juvenile Naturalist*, by
the Rev B H. Draper, 1839, sets the scene for many works of a similar
kind. The study of nature was not only improving in itself but it could
usefully occupy the period of time when other formal instruction had been
laid aside, and it also fulfilled that other object dear to eighteenth- and
nineteenth-century educators, of using everything as a means of instruction,
especially in the daily walks which took the place of much of the modern
child's playtime. There were many books on botany for the young, which
was definitely a 'doing' subject, in a way which the study of birds, however
useful and popular, could not be. The keeping of pets, more easily accom-
plished in the days of large houses and gardens – and servants to clear up –
was also recommended by some writers. Looking after animals too could
be turned to good account and the young child would thus learn to consider
the wants of another creature so dependent on him:

A child of a benevolent and affectionate disposition, will here find full
scope for exercising many amiable qualities, and will hardly fail of
regarding with feelings of lively interest, the creatures that he cherishes,

and which are so entirely dependent on his care for the supply of their several necessities.

Above:
137 THE PURGATORY OF PETER THE CRUEL by James Greenwood. Illustrated by Ernest Griset. George Routledge & Sons, 1868. 22 × 19 cm. Peter behaved cruelly to living creatures. It was his fate, therefore, to be changed into the shape of some of his former victims. In this picture he is the fly about to be impaled on the fisherman's hook.

Opposite top:
138 THE NEWTONIAN SYSTEM OF PHILOSOPHY . . . by Tom Telescope. A new edition . . . by William Magnet. Ogilvy and Speare, 1794. 13 × 8 cm. A work first published in 1761 under the title *The Philosophy of Tops and Balls*. In this edition, it has been brought up to date by the inclusion of the first balloon flight across the Channel in 1785.

Opposite bottom:
139 WHAT MAKES ME GROW? OR, WALKS AND TALKS WITH AMY DUDLEY. . . . With . . . illustrations by Lorenz Fröhlich. Seeley, Jackson & Halliday, 1875. 18 × 13 cm. An experiment with the wind to explain how the lungs work.

writes the author in *Sketches from Nature*, 1830. To judge by its frequent mention in the writings of the period, cruelty to animals, birds and insects must have been very prevalent among the young. It was a point brought up constantly, not only in books dealing specifically with the subject but also in books on moral improvement and similar topics. Indeed, a 'Mr Frankly' went so far as to write at great length on the subject in *The Trial of Harry Hardheart; for Ingratitude and Cruelty to Certain Individuals of the Brute Creation, c.* 1820. A similar theme in the hands of a great artist could be quite terrifying or gruesome, as we see in *The Purgatory of Peter the Cruel*, by James Greenwood, 1868, illustrated by Ernest Griset.

While the keeping of pets and the study of botany or shells was recommended for juvenile study, it is interesting for us to note that generally there was little suggestion of home scientific experiments, or even very much on pure science at all until towards the end of the nineteenth century; it was not, of course, a subject normally studied in school in the early part of the century, nor was it one whose results fitted comfortably into the idea of the universe as the adult liked to portray it to the young. There was, of course, the inevitable 'Peter Parley': *Peter Parley's Tales About the Sun, Moon and Stars* (3ed. 1838) and *Papa's Tales About the Sun and Stars, c.* 1845. Some attempt to popularize scientific matters was made in such works as *The Three Useful Giants: Wind, Water and Steam, and What They Do For Us*, published by Dean & Son in 'toy-book' format, while others like William Martin's *Fireside Philosophy; or, Home Science*, 1845, not only pointed the way to the future, but also provided a link with one of the earliest works of this nature. This was *The Newtonian System of Philosophy: Adapted to the Capacities of Young Ladies and Gentlemen, and Familiarized and made Entertaining by Objects with which They are Intimately Acquainted* by Tom Telescope, 1794. In this the scientific knowledge of the period was explained from everyday objects, the spinning top for the talk on motion, or the wheel heating against the brake as the chaise went downhill and so on.

It was of course accepted that children would demand explanations of things in the world around them and a number of compilations set out to satisfy this demand. Such a work was *Glimpses of the Wonderful*, a Christmas annual that appeared in 1845 and offered information on a number of subjects, from tiger hunting to steam ships. 'Wonderful' appears to have been a favourite adjective of the mid-Victorians and it appears again in *A History of Wonderful Inventions*, 1849, which dealt with subjects like the mariner's compass, gas light, and the electric telegraph. Other scientific writings for children show the influence of the prevailing Victorian fondness for the facetious approach, as in *The Fairy Tales of Science*, 1859, by J. C. Brough, illustrated by C. H. Bennett; in this the author sought to clothe science 'in the more attractive garb of fairy tale'. Well-known writers such as Charles Kingsley also produced works of scientific or natural history interest for children; his *Madam How and Lady Why; or, First Lessons in Earth Lore for Children*, 1870, first appeared in a periodical *Good Words for the Young*. The nineteenth century saw a great increase in juvenile magazines in which much specialized information often appeared; *The Boy's Own Paper* was a good example of this kind of journal. The earlier magazines for children had often contained items on natural history but only in a very general way. *The Boy's Own Paper*, first published in 1879, included, in addition to such items as serialized tales, discussions on hobbies and correspondence, scientific articles of a straightforward nature as well as short items on natural history. Few works of any kind, however, concerned themselves with human physiology, and a book like *What Makes Me Grow? or, Walks and Talks with Amy Dudley*, 1875, which was written for quite small children, was one of the few that attempted this subject.

When it came to the illustration of books on natural history in all its various branches, there was great diversity of approach. It was a subject in which illustration could be 'pretty-pretty' or purely technical. Accuracy in representation was not the first requirement in spite of the high standard set by the wood engravings of Bewick in the late eighteenth and early nineteenth centuries. Many of the hack artists employed on this type of work were technically ignorant and it was not considered necessary to be meticulous in the production of children's books, even though some fine volumes on natural history were being published for adults: for example the work of the American, J. J. Audubon (1785–1851), and the Frenchman P. J. Redouté's books on flowers. Certainly higher standards of accuracy developed with the nineteenth century and we find books full of diagrammatic drawings of flowers and their parts, of shells, of insects and various other natural phenomena. With such drawings went fairly solid textual matter although it might be disguised in the form of conversation. But at the same time, the romantic approach continued to be employed, even in the most serious-minded book. Thus for example one might find good technical drawings in the text, but the plates might show an only marginally related scene, perhaps even highly coloured, of, say, children in a field or garden, often with birds or animals out of all proportion in size to the human figures depicted. Flowers always lent themselves to attractive illustration, and flower painting was an art considered particularly suited to ladies. An interesting feature of continental flower books was their fondness for personification. This was less common in English-language books in which a practical approach seems to have been much more usual. As a result we get such works as those by Louise Leneveux *Les Fleurs Parlantes*, 1848, and *Les Petis Habitants des Fleurs, c.* 1845. The illustrations were hand-coloured but the development of colour printing in the middle years of the nineteenth century opened the door to a whole flood of natural history books, if some of the rather lightweight works can be given that epithet. These were the nursery books of the kind we still know today. *The*

56   *Of the Air, Atmosphere, &c.*

event of Mr. Blanchard and Dr. Jefferies crossing the English Channel from Dover to France.

I am surprised at so simple a question, says our philosopher. Why, surely, you never considered the reason of those balls that I have seen you make by soap and water beat to a lather, and blown out of the bowl of a tobacco-pipe! The air by which they are blown, issuing from your lungs, is specifically lighter than the common air, even when contained in that thin watery globe. Now, inflammable air is about

140 SEASIDE WALKS OF A NATURALIST WITH HIS CHILDREN by the Rev. W. Houghton. New edition. Groombridge & Sons, 1889. 18 × 12 cm. In addition to wood engravings of the type shown here, this book has a few attractive colour plates, showing the subjects in their natural surroundings. This double-page spread shows the mixture of romantic and technical illustration which frequently characterized this type of book.

tacles, the mouth being situated in the centre of the flower. I will suddenly move the glass jar; do you see every little creature has withdrawn itself into its cell? the flowers are all gone, and the alcyon

ALCYONIUM DIGITATUM.

is nothing but an apparently dead mass. Imbedded in this fleshy mass are a number of curious bodies called *spicula*. You cannot see them without the help of a good microscope; but if I were to cut a

SPICULES OF ALCYONIUM.

thin slice off this mass, lay it on a glass slip, with a little caustic potass to dissolve the fleshy portion, and put it under the microscope, I should see these calcareous spicules. The specimen before us is a small

one. Alcyonium loves deep water, from whence v large specimens may be obtained by dredging. T are generally attached to old oyster-shells. W a number of jelly-fish the retiring waters have behind them! they look very uninteresting now, it is a beautiful sight to see them on a calm summ day to watch their movements in the water; we pay attention to them on another occasion.

Now is it pleasant in the summer-eve,
When a broad shore retiring waters leave,
Awhile to wait upon the fine fair sand
When all is calm at sea, all still on land;
And there the ocean's produce to explore
As floating by, or rolling on the shore;
Those living jellies which the flesh inflame
Fierce as a nettle, and from that their name;
Some in huge masses, some that you may bring
In the small compass of a lady's ring;
Figured by Hand Divine—there's not a gem
Wrought by man's art to be compared to them-
Soft, brilliant, tender, through the wave they glow
And make the moonbeam brighter where they flow.

Child's Picture Book of Domestic Animals, published by Routledge in 1869 and *Buttercups and Daisies and Other Pretty Flowers,* published about the same time, were typical. The plates were usually highly coloured representations of animals, flowers, birds or insects, with either straightforward descriptions or perhaps short verses; although the primary intention was to give information of a kind, the texts were not regarded in the same serious way as in the various books on other subjects we have considered. They were primarily picture books with accompanying words and, although the best accurately represented their subjects, the worst could be just as misleading as their modern counterparts.

Of all the subjects we have considered in this book, natural history is surely one which, together with the alphabet books, brings the modern child closest to his predecessors. The cats and the dogs, the cows, the flowers and the birds, all are the same as they were to the eighteenth- or nineteenth-century child, cautiously exploring the living world around him, wondering and questioning. The photograph has still not entirely superseded the observant eye and the clever pencil. Though our attitude to the world of nature has changed from that of our ancestors and our knowledge likewise, the young can disregard such matters even as children of an earlier period could ignore the religious and didactic fare they were offered. The true miracle of growth and life and colour has remained unchanged for them throughout the centuries.

11 Grammar

Grammar is one of the most difficult subjects to illustrate – indeed one might be forgiven for considering it impossible. It has always been an unpalatable subject for children – and for adults, as many who have tried to learn a foreign language would agree. For this very reason it was in particular need of help from illustration. Leaving aside the pure textbook, there seem to have been two methods of approach: one was to personify the parts of speech, to illustrate them, and then often to accompany them with verse. *Punctuation Personified* by 'Mr Stops', was a very successful example of this kind, being clearly and memorably illustrated in both picture and verse. *Sir Hornbook*, on the other hand, was surely less successful. It was written by Thomas Love Peacock and first published, anonymously, in 1814. The idea was ingenious, as explained by the title *Sir Hornbook; or, Childe Launcelot's Expedition. A Grammatico-Allegorical Ballad*, but the execution of the idea in verse made the grammatical allusions so involved that the child must have been even more confused at the end. Here is one of the easier passages:

> They swam the moat, they scal'd the wall,
> Sir VERB, with rage and shame,
> Beheld his valiant *general* fall,
> INFINITIVE by name[1].

> INDICATIVE *declar'd* the foes[2]
> Should perish by his hand;
> And stout IMPERATIVE arose[3],
> The squadron to *command*.

While such a book *may* have helped some children to remember their grammar, it cannot have had the impact of 'Mr Stops'.

Another method of treating the subject of grammar was one eminently suited to the Victorian taste, which delighted in the facetious. Such books could be quite successful, since amusing figures adjacent to simple text could be retained in the mind when straightforward explanations had failed to gain a foothold. Allied to this approach was the one which endeavoured to make the subject into a game. Julia Corner's *Play Grammar* was an example, but the text is stodgy and good results may well be doubted. For the most part grammar lessons must always have been left mainly to school, or at least to the schoolroom, for although many parents might feel competent to teach reading, counting or spelling, technical grammar was perhaps beyond most of them – as indeed it would be for many of us today!

"The ducks swim in the pond, low and the willow bends its long branches, to shade them from the hot sun."

"Now, for the nouns," said Herbert; "*ducks, pond, willow, branches,* and *sun.*"

"Very well, Herbert, those are all the nouns."

"Yes, mamma, and the verbs are *swim*; I can swim, you know; so that must be a verb; but I don't see any more."

"Then I am afraid you will have to pay me a forfeit, Herbert, for there are two more verbs."

141 THE PLAY GRAMMAR; OR, ELEMENTS OF GRAMMAR EXPLAINED IN EASY GAMES by Miss Corner. 9ed. Thomas Dean & Son [*c.* 1855]. 16 × 10 cm. This was an attempt to render the learning of English grammar more attractive to children, but the result was rather ponderous.

---

[1] The INFINITIVE mood expresses a thing in a *general* and unlimited manner: as, '*To love, to walk, to be ruled.*'
[2] The INDICATIVE mood simply *indicates* or *declares* a thing: as, 'He loves:' 'he is loved:' or asks a question: as, 'Does he love?' – 'Is he loved?'
[3] The IMPERATIVE mood *commands* or *entreats*: as, 'Depart:' 'Come hither:' – 'Forgive me.'

THIS IS *what* HE WANTED; THAT IS TO SAY, *the thing which* HE WANTED.

That is applied to both *persons* and *things*; as,

HE *that* ACTS WISELY DESERVES PRAISE.

Above:

142 THE PICTORIAL GRAMMAR by Alfred Crowquill. Harvey & Darton [1842]. 16 × 11 cm. A perfectly straightforward grammar book illustrated by 'Alfred Crowquill'. It was not the pictures themselves that provided the humour so much as their juxtaposition with the text.

Above right:

143 THE TOY GRAMMAR; OR, LEARNING WITHOUT LABOUR. T. Dean & Son [*c.* 1855]. (Merriment series; Sister Lady-bird series). 24 × 16 cm. A typical example of the humorous illustration found in books for both children and adults in the middle years of the nineteenth century. Unfortunately the rather muddled layout of this page detracts from its praiseworthy attempt to make the subject more palatable. The woodcuts have been crudely hand-coloured.

Nevertheless, it was among the grammar books that two of the most attractive early instructional works were to be found. They came from that great purveyor of the home educational book, John Harris, and were published in 1824. Both could perhaps be used today, since they are attractive, simple and memorable – and what more could be required of a grammar book? Perhaps the better known is *Punctuation Personified; or, Pointing Made Easy* by Mr Stops. The other is *The Infant's Grammar; or, the Pic-nic Party of the Parts of Speech.* Certainly the page illustrated in plate 130, which was hand-coloured in the original, gives a very good explanation of pronouns, and explains them in a form that a child might well remember – or a parent teach.

In the plate 143 taken from *The Toy Grammar; or, Learning Without Labour, c.* 1855, though an amusing exposition of a difficult theme, the general muddle of the layout tends to confuse an already involved subject. The humour would probably appeal more to an adult than a young child.

2 *The Pictorial Grammar* by Alfred Crowquill, 1842, offered quite straight-forward instruction but the humorous illustrations made an impact by their unexpectedness. The text could have been used in schools as well as at home, but it is unlikely that the illustrations would have permitted its employment in the classroom. After all, in the example which accompanied the explanation of the word 'that', *viz* 'He that acts wisely deserves praise', the boy is running *away* from the man who has fallen through the ice – this suggests more the attitude of an Edward Lear than the high moral tone to be found in school books of the period.

1 Besides Miss Corner's *Play Grammar*, which went into several editions – perhaps because it made few concessions to amusement or real humour –

LE VERBE **PRONOMINAL** EST CELUI QUI SE CONJUGUE AVEC DEUX PRONOMS DE LA MÊME PERSONNE.

Exemple : tu vois bien, Émile, TU T'AMUSES, TU T'EN REPENTIRAS papa SE FÂCHERA contre toi

144 GRAMMAIRE DROLATIQUE (Humorous Grammar) by M. Hamley, Paris [*c.* 1865?]. 16 × 26 cm. The success of this attempt to illustrate the grammatical points may well be doubted, since there is not a very obvious link between the text and the pictures.[1] The competent tinted lithographs of the book compare favourably with the cruder contemporary woodcuts of English children's books, but their use put up the cost.

[1] You will see Émile, if you play now, you will be sorry –
Papa will be cross with you.

other similar attempts were made to involve games and tales. One that was rather more successful, because it made its points more clearly, was *The Little Grammarian; or, An Easy Guide to the Parts of Speech . . . in a Series of Instructive and Amusing Tales*, 1828. The following is the end of a story taken from the section on 'Articles':

> At length, her mother said to her husband, 'Did you not hear her say *the* man? Now by that she must mean some one in particular; if she had said *a* man, I should have thought some silly fellow or other had been playing tricks with *the* child. Surely, John, she has not seen *the* man who lamed and robbed you?' 'I have, I have, mother,' said little Ann. . . .
>
> The consequence was, that John hastened to *the* Plough as fast as his crippled limbs would enable him, and arrived there just in time to recognize and secure *the* man who had assaulted and robbed him, before he departed. . . . Now, had little Ann used *a* instead of *the* in her alarm; *the* thief would have escaped before she had been able to tell her parents what she really meant: hence learn the great difference between *a* or *an* and *the*.

The difficulty of making grammar attractive and illustrating it suitably was not by any means confined to English-language works. A work like the *Grammaire Drôlatique*, by M. Hamley, *c.* 1865?, was a French grammar where text and illustrations were not very well integrated. Such illustrations, which were reproduced by the lithographic method more commonly used in continental books, *may* have helped to memorize grammatical points, but in spite of its title it lacked any lightness of touch to help the child along. That the subject could be dealt with satisfactorily is proved by Walter Crane's *Grammar in Rhyme*, 1868, an ideal home-learning book. Here the intention was not so much to impart the solid fare that would be taught at school but rather to give a general idea of the subject. The rhymes were brief and memorable, and the pictures, while works of art in themselves, were perfectly relevant. Moreover, this particular 'toy book' lacked the clutter of detail which sometimes spoilt Crane's illustration. In spite of the difficulty of illustrating the subject at all, some books conveyed their message successfully and they are the ones that would be as effective today.

12 Music

The playing of a musical instrument, being essentially a practical subject, might not be considered suitable for the type of illustration with which this work is concerned. Indeed, how should one set about making music pictorial? This is something which has still not been solved today, although teachers are still experimenting; a recent German book[1] makes an interesting comparison with those of an earlier century. In the two hundred years covered in this book music in the home was an extremely important part of leisure. It was considered a standard accomplishment of every young lady that she should have some musical proficiency, and in the long winter evenings at home all were expected to take their part in the family musical entertainment.

But music is not entirely a matter of practical performance; the rudiments of theory had to be learned and it was here that the opportunity for illustration presented itself. Those children who were allowed help from illustrated books would have been familiar with *The Gamut and Time-Table in Verse*, a work that had a long vogue and appeared in many forms, with or without acknowledgment to the original author. Two versions are illustrated in plates 145 and 146, only one of which bears the author's name. The illustrations have been updated in the later edition and this extended to a change in the instrument itself.

Another method of assisting the learner with musical theory is to be found in a work entitled *The Juvenile Pianist; or, A Mirror of Music for Infant Minds*, by Anne Rodwell, 1836. This uses the well-tried conversational method, although, as so often, the child makes small contribution to the talk, beyond seeking information. Dialogue from *The Juvenile Pianist* runs as follows:

MAMMA.

Good morning to you my dear, I did not expect to find you here at this early hour.

HARRIETT.

I have made all the haste I could Mamma, that you might have time to tell me about the Marks Composers use in Music.

MAMMA.

Oh then, I find you have not forgotten my promise, nor have I; for see I have brought you a nice little Music Slate; as I thought you would like to make the different characters on it, as I describe them.

Information on musical subjects might be included in more general works. *The New Picture Book* by Nicholas Bohny could have been included in several other chapters of the present book – it is referred to, for example, in the chapter on 'Counting' – but it is illustrated here to show how

23

With F, on the fifth line; so do not forget

This lesson of lines and of spaces I've set,

Which when you've repeated as well as

you're able,

We'll pass to the next rule, they call the

Time-table.

145 THE GAMUT AND TIME-TABLE IN VERSE FOR THE INSTRUCTION OF CHILDREN, by C. Finch. A. K. Newman & Co. [1820?]. 17 × 10 cm. Verses were a popular form of instruction, especially when illustrated. Often later editions of books like this were published without acknowledgement to the author (see plate 146).

---

[1] *Bunte Zaubernoten* [etc.], by M. Neuhäser, 1965.

LEDGER LINES.

G A B C D   G A B C D E F G A B C

F G A B C D E F   B C D E F

And now, dear Maria, I wish to explain,
That the line we call Ledger, is only a name
For a line that is *added*, above or below:
Its uses in Music you'll presently know;
Without it, good lessons could not well be set.
That Ledger means added, you will not forget.

musical instruction might be included in books which covered a wider
educational field.

Music was obviously a good field for private enterprise and experimenta-
tion, since several of the home teaching books which have would-be helpful
illustrations are private productions. Their authors no doubt sought to
popularize a method which had been successfully used among their own
children. *Old Semibreve* was probably issued privately, but its ability to
teach quickly is hardly obvious. Since music is continuous in time perhaps
illustrative methods could not really hope to succeed in teaching until the
advent of television.

IN THE POLE SKREEN.

FIRST line of music, left hand, B is to be played twice over. Second line, the transient shake. Third line, the scale of C major, with thirds marked. Fourth line, the chords of C major, and Da Capo from the beginning.

IN THE OTTOMAN.

FIRST line, left hand, the Rests, in the first six bars; seventh bar, clef note treble. Second line, first bar, clef note bass; second bar, a semitone; third bar, a tone; fourth bar, a double sharp; fifth bar, a double flat; sixth bar, a semibreve with a dot. Third line, first bar, a dotted crotchet; second bar, three minims; third bar, three quavers; fourth bar, legato played smoothly; fifth bar, moderately staccato. Fourth line, first bar, staccato; second bar, crescendo and diminuendo. Fifth line, first bar, A sharp; second bar, A flat; third bar, A natural.

The Pole Skreen is ornamented with the leaves of the Lily of the Valley and Geranium.

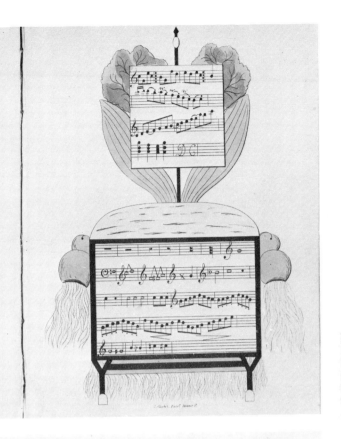

How many of these soldiers blow the trumpet? How many play the fife? How many beat the drum? (8 = 3 + 3 + 2, or 8 = 2 times 3 + 2.) Of what material is the trumpet made? of what the fife? Wherein are they alike? Wherein unlike? What do you hear when these instruments are blown? Are the notes equally high; deep, long, short?

13 Languages

Few publications tried to teach foreign languages by means of pictures. This is surprising when we remember that the first real picture book for children was intended for this very purpose. Comenius' *Orbis Sensualium Pictus*, published in 1658, was designed to teach children Latin; it is incidentally full of scenes and objects from daily life. The text consists of parallel sentences in Latin and the vernacular. It was translated into English by Charles Hoole in 1659 and long remained popular. It had many imitators, one of whom was James Greenwood who, in *London Vocabulary* (1771), used many of the illustrations that are to be found in Hoole's work. Already out of date in 1771, to many juvenile readers they must have seemed quite as archaic then as they would appear to children today. On the whole the detailed description of objects and trades, as given in the work of Comenius and his followers, was not the method used in the books published for helping to teach languages at home. The main aim of the later books seems to have been the development of conversational fluency, together with a reasonable vocabulary of everyday words – grammar could be left to the schoolroom.

Comenius' work was intended primarily as a schoolbook to teach Latin, but on the whole Latin was rarely taught informally and will therefore concern us little here. 'Learning' was for a long time classical learning and the teaching of such a subject was a more serious matter than the acquisition of modern languages, at least in the eyes of many educationalists. Only one book shown here attempted a little preliminary teaching of Latin and

[1] *Orbis pictus: a facsimile of the first English edition of 1659.* Introduced by J. E. Sadler, London, O.U.P., 1968.

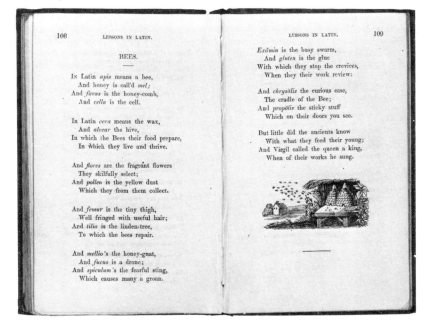

149 PRETTY LESSONS IN VERSE FOR GOOD CHILDREN, WITH SOME LESSONS IN LATIN IN EASY RHYME by Sara Coleridge. 3rd edition. J. W. Parker, 1839. 14 × 10 cm. One of the few books which attempted to teach Latin to the very young; it contains some related illustrations.

Top:

150 ORBIS SENSUALIUM PICTUS . . . JOH. AMOS COMENIUS'S VISIBLE WORLD; OR, A NOMENCLATURE, AND PICTURES OF ALL THE CHIEF THINGS THAT ARE IN THE WORLD, AND OF MEN'S EMPLOYMENT THEREIN. . . . 12ed. Translated into English by Charles Hoole, for S. Leacroft, 1777. 16×10 cm. First translated into English in 1659, this was one of the earliest picture books for children and so marks an important development in teaching methods.

Bottom:

151 LE BABILLARD, AN AMUSING INTRODUCTION TO THE FRENCH LANGUAGE by a French lady. 2ed. J. Harris, 1834. 13×11 cm. The 'French lady' of the title was in fact M. J. G. de la Voye, a professional teacher; his work went into a number of editions.

11

Le Ca-ba-ret.

Mon thé est chaud.

Je ne puis pas le boire.

Il se-ra bien-tôt froid.

Ne le ré-pan-dez pas.

Vous n'au-rez plus de thé, si vous le ré-pan-dez.

Pre-nez du pain, et un peu de beurre.

152 LA BAGATELLE: INTENDED TO INTRODUCE CHILDREN OF THREE OR FOUR YEARS OLD TO SOME KNOWLEDGE OF THE FRENCH LANGUAGE by N.L. New edition, 2 vols. in 1. For Baldwin & Cradock, 1829. 14 × 8 cm. This work, intended to encourage French conversation in very young children, was re-issued over many years. Eventually the illustrations had to be modernized (see plate 153).

although it may have helped the child acquire a very elementary vocabulary, it offered nothing further. French and German were the preoccupations of most of the home teaching language books.

For British people French was the obvious first foreign language: the language of fashion, culture and diplomacy, maintaining its importance even during periods of hostility between the two countries. Paris was one of the first stops on the Englishman's Grand Tour of Europe and the nearest big city in which to enjoy all the delights of a foreign country without being too far from home. In addition to books for beginners, there was a number of works in French intended for children who had already acquired a certain reading ability in the language. They might be published in France and imported, or written in England, translated into French and published in either country. Mrs Barbauld and Mrs Trimmer were among well-known English authors to be published in both languages and countries, as well as writers of short novels for the young, such as Mrs Hofland, whose work lies outside the scope of the present book. Such books were often given as presents to English-speaking children, as inscriptions within the books prove. Perhaps it helped to read in a foreign language a story already familiar in the vernacular.

During part of the period we are considering, a number of indigent émigrés from revolutionary and post-revolutionary France found that their one chance of earning money might be by teaching their own language. In this way interest in things French was kept alive in both Britain and America, where a number of exiles found refuge. One of the most popular home teaching books was *La Bagatelle* by 'Madame N.L.', first published in 1801. As with the much earlier Comenius, we can learn from it a great deal about contemporary life, and it also followed its predecessor in giving an everyday type of vocabulary; its short sentences of conversation, however, were not of the kind to be found in the earlier work. *La Bagatelle* proved very popular, and subsequently had to be revised, especially as far as the pictures were concerned (the text was only slightly altered). A similar type of work was *Le Babillard*, again with simple sentences and a vocabulary firmly anchored in daily life. M. Aublay's *The French Present; or, Easy Dialogues, French and English, Adapted to the Capacities of Young Beginners*, 1813, also went into numerous editions.

Once past the very simple stage, the young learner might hope for something more interesting than limited conversation. Maria Hack's *Histoires Intéressantes de Quelques Animaux, pour la Lecture Française de Jeunes Enfans* (Interesting stories about some animals for reading in French by young children), 1839, certainly offered well-illustrated information on natural history subjects, but it must have been quite difficult reading for 'jeunes enfans'. Other authors also felt that the opportunity should be taken to offer more than just a language, and so we get French moral tales of the sort to be found in *Les Hochets Moraux; ou, Contes pour la Première Enfance* by Monget, 1806. In the preface to this work the publisher stated that it was intended to offer 'à la jeunesse angloise une nouvelle avec une augmentation de quatrains qui développement la morale de chaque conte, et qui par le moyen des tableaux qui peignent les différentes passions, en facilitent aux jeunes lecteurs l'intelligence et leur but moral'.[1] Another writer, hiding herself under the anonymity of 'Par une dame', suggested that a language would be better remembered if it were not associated only with the hours of learning. To this end the child should be encouraged to use its knowledge in both work and play, and for this she published *Les Jeux de la Jeunesse; ou, Nouvelle Méthode à Instruire les Enfans, en les Amusant par la Représentation des Differens Jeux et Exercices du Corps. . . . Avec des Explications sur les Avantages ou les Dangers qui peuvent Résulter pour leur Santé de ces Jeux et Exercices.*[2] We may well wonder how many children were prepared to accept her versions of popular children's games!

In spite of a general interest shown in Italian art, and the fact that Italy was frequently included in the Grand Tour, there was little interest in teaching children Italian. Many of the visitors to Italy were much more interested in its early Roman history than with the country's more recent past; the classical education enjoyed by most people ensured this familiarity. Even in the nineteenth century, when English-speaking colonies grew

[1] 'to the youth of England a tale with the addition of verses which develop the moral of each story, and which by means of illustrations, depict the various passions to make clear to young readers both the meaning and the moral point'.

[2] *Games of Childhood; or, A New Method of Teaching Children by Entertaining them with Pictures of Different Games and Exercises . . . with Explanations on the Advantages or Dangers which may Result to their Health from Such Games and Exercises.*

Le ca-ba-ret.

Mon thé est trop chaud.

Je ne puis pas le boire.

Il se-ra bien-tôt moins chaud.

Ne le ré-pan-dez pas.

Vous n'au-rez plus de thé si vous le ré-pan-dez.

Pre-nez du pain, et un peu de beurre.

14

Der Herr.

THE GENTLEMAN.

Ich bitte beschreiben Sie mir den Herrn, der da so bequem zu sitzen scheint.

Describe, I beg of you, that gentleman who seems sitting there so comfortably.

Dies ist sein Anzug,	This is his dress,
er trägt	he wears
einen blauen Rock,	a blue coat,
ein weißes Halstuch,	a white cravat,
eine farbige Weste,	a colored waistcoat,
graue Beinkleider,	grey trowsers,
baumwollene Strümpfe,	cotton stockings,
Stiefel,	boots,
ein feines Hemde,	a fine shirt,
einen braunen Ueberrock,	a brown overcoat,
ein seidenes Schnupftuch,	a silk pocket-handker-chief,

Der Herr.

THE GENTLEMAN.

Above:

153 LA BAGATELLE: INTENDED TO INTRODUCE CHILDREN OF FIVE OR SIX YEARS OLD TO SOME KNOWLEDGE OF THE FRENCH LANGUAGE by N.L. New edition. Lockwood & Co., 1871. 14 × 9 cm. A later edition of this work, it should be compared with plate 152. The illustrations have been brought up to date and provide an interesting comment on changes in taste since the early part of the century. A few alterations were also made in the text, and the ages specified in the title were increased.

Left:

154 DER SCHWÄTZER: AN AMUSING INTRODUCTION TO THE GERMAN LANGUAGE. Griffith & Farran, 1858. 13 × 10 cm. A German version of *Le Babillard* (plate 151) using the same text and illustrations, which by this date were very old fashioned.

155 ZWEEN BETTELKNABEN: EINE LEHRREICHE GESCHICHTE FÜR UMSERE DEUTSCHEN KINDER. NEBST ZWO TODESGESCHICHTEN (Two Beggar Boys: an Improving Tale for our German Children. Also Two Stories about Death). Philadelphia, Heinrich Schweitzer etc., 1806. 13.5 cm. Books in foreign languages were required for children reaching America from continental Europe – a fact which had to be taken into account even more as the nineteenth century progressed. The content of this work could be parallelled in many similar pious tracts for English-speaking children: the episode illustrated is called 'the holy death of Maria'.

up in various towns in the peninsula, there was on the whole little interest in Italian in the schoolroom. German, too, was little regarded, in spite of the German origin of the House of Hanover and the fact that up to the accession of Queen Victoria in 1837 the sovereign was also King of Hanover. However at the end of the Napoleonic wars England and the German states found themselves allied against France, and suspicion of the future activities of France led to continued links even after the restoration of the Bourbons. Contacts were further strengthened by the Prince Consort's partiality for things connected with the land of his birth and, later, by the marriage of the Princess Royal to the heir to the Prussian throne. German instructional books followed the pattern set by Comenius and *La Bagatelle*. One publisher went so far as to issue the same work in both French and German languages: entitled *Le Babillard* in French and *Der Schwätzer* in German. The pattern of the text was the same, as were the illustrations, so that the fashions must have appeared extremely dated in the German version of 1858. In America, however, more foreign language books were published in view of the people of different nationalities who settled there throughout the nineteenth century. A typical work for German-speaking American children is illustrated in plate 155.

But of course the best way to learn a foreign language is to do so from a native speaker; therefore those who could afford it employed a French or German governess for their children, and we find this character making her appearance in many contemporary books for children. Perhaps they are her marks which we can still see in some of the books intended for her pupils: a faint pencilled date showing the progress made so far and, occasionally, a child's name against it, as various members of the family began their struggle with an unfamiliar tongue.

In the form of a post-script

This book does not come to a neat end; each of the chapters is largely self-contained and the number could be increased to cover even more of the subjects on which books for the young have been written. Nevertheless, there *is* something to be said in conclusion. In collecting material for *Cobwebs to Catch Flies* I have looked through some thousands of children's books; but far more exist than have been consulted for this study; the Renier Collection alone amounts to more than 45,000 items. Only a few could be mentioned or illustrated in this book without making it a mere list of titles. For those wishing to pursue the subject further, a bibliography follows. It includes some additional titles of children's books not mentioned in the main text. Many of these can be found in larger libraries with specialist collections of children's books; all of them are in the National Art Library, Victoria and Albert Museum, London.

The short list of books on the history of juvenile literature mentions only the most important works on the subject, since they contain good bibliographies which should be consulted by anyone studying children's books. A certain amount of background reading on the history and social conditions of the period covered by *Cobwebs* is also included. But the most important way to understand or study children's books is to read as many of them as possible – for this there is no substitute. It is hoped that the fragmentary quotations contained in this work will encourage readers to seek out the originals (many of which are being reprinted) and discover for themselves the pleasure to be found in these old books intended for the 'little masters and misses' of long ago.

Bibliography

This bibliography is divided into two sections. The first section contains books on the history and other aspects of early children's books, and is itself divided into two: English-language books and foreign books. Many of the works quoted themselves contain useful bibliographies with which to supplement reading on aspects of early children's books.

The second section contains lists of children's books related to chapters of the present work; for the most part, they are among the better known of their kind. For those readers who do not have access to such books, a reading of the titles alone is revealing, but lists of them would be out of place in the main body of the work. For the serious student, they may provide a guide to other children's books in the same field, to be found in some of the collections listed on p. 149. The date and place of publication of the books in this section are those of copies in the Victoria and Albert Museum, London, which are not necessarily first editions. The books are listed alphabetically by title, since many children's books were published anonymously, especially at their first appearance.

IN ENGLISH

1 Books on early children's books

Aston, J., *Chapbooks of the eighteenth century*. London, Chatto & Windus, 1882.

Darton, F. J. H., *Children's books in England: five centuries of social life*. 2ed. Cambridge, CUP, 1958.

Earle, A. M., *Child life in colonial days*. New York, Macmillan, 1899.

Egoff, S. A., *Children's periodicals of the 19th century: a survey and a bibliography*. London, Library Association, 1951.

Field, L. F., *The child and his book*. London, Wells, Gardner, Darton & Co., 1891.

Folmsbee, B., *A little history of the horn-book*. 3rd printing. Boston, Horn Book Inc., 1965.

Grafton & Co., *A collection of horn books . . . in ivory, wood, silver and brass etc*. The whole offered for sale by G. & Co., 1923.

Green, R. L., *Tellers of tales: children's books and their authors from 1800–1964*. Rev. ed. London, E. Ward, 1965.

Harvey, W., *Scottish chapbook literature*. Paisley, A. Gardner, 1903.

Hindley, C., *The history of the Catnach Press* [etc.]. London, C. Hindley, 1886.

Hindley, C., *The life and times of James Catnach*. (Facsimile reprint.) Welwyn Garden City, Seven Dials Press, 1970.

Horn Book Magazine. Boston, 1924–.

Illustrators of children's books. I. 1744–1845. Compiled by B. Mahony. Boston, Horn Book Inc., 1927.

Jaeger, M., *Before Victoria: changing standards and behaviour, 1787–1837*. Harmondsworth, Penguin Books, 1967.

Johnson, C., *Old time schools and school-books*. New York, Dover Press, 1963 (reprint of 1904 ed.).

King, A., and Stuart, A. F., *The house of Warne: one hundred years of publishing*. London, Warne, 1965.

King-Hall, M., *The story of the nursery*. London, Routledge & Kegan Paul, 1958.

Library of Congress, Washington,	*Children's literature: a guide to reference sources.* Compiled by V. Haviland. Washington, 1966.
MacLean, R.,	*Pictorial alphabets.* London, Studio Vista, 1969.
	Victorian book design and colour printing. 2ed. London, Faber, 1972.
Merritt, P.,	*The royal primer.* (Reprinted from: *Bibliographical essays: a tribute to Wilberforce Eames.*) Cambridge, 1925.
Muir, M.,	*A bibliography of Australian children's books.* London, Deutsch, 1970.
Muir, P.,	*English children's books, 1600 to 1900.* London, Batsford, 1954 (reprinted 1969).
National Book League, London,	*Children's books of yesterday.* London, 1946.
Neuburg, V.,	*Chapbooks: a bibliography of references to English and American chapbook literature of the eighteenth and nineteenth centuries.* London, 1964.
Opie, I. and P.,	*The Oxford dictionary of nursery rhymes.* Oxford, OUP, 1969.
Pearson, E.,	*Banbury chapbooks and nursery toy book literature of the XVIII and early XIX centuries.* (Facsimile reprint.) Welwyn Garden City, Seven Dials Press, 1970.
Pinchbeck, I., and Hewitt, M.,	*Children in English society.* 2 vols. London, Routledge & Kegan Paul, 1969–73.
Quayle, E.,	*The collector's book of children's books.* London, Studio Vista, 1971.
Roe, F. G.,	*The Victorian child.* London, Phoenix House, 1959.
	The Georgian child. London, Phoenix House, 1961.
Roscoe, S.,	*John Newbery and his successors, 1740–1814: a bibliography.* Wormley, Five Owls Press. 1973.
Rosenbach, A. S. W.,	*Early American children's books.* Portland, Maine, The Southworth Press, 1933.
Smith, J. A.,	*Children's illustrated books.* (Britain in pictures: the British people in pictures.) London, Collins, 1948.
Spielman, M. H.,	*Kate Greenaway.* London, A. & C. Black, 1905.
Thwaite, M. F.,	*From primer to pleasure in reading: an introduction to the history of children's books in England.* 2ed. London, The Library Association, 1972.
Toronto, Public Library,	*The Osborne collection of early children's books, 1566–1910: a catalogue.* Prepared . . . by J. St John. Toronto, 1966.
Tuer, A. W.,	*The history of the horn-book.* 2 vols. London, Leadenhall Press, 1896.
	Stories and pictures from forgotten children's books. London, Leadenhall Press, 1898–99.
	Stories from old-fashioned children's books. London, Leadenhall Press, 1899–1900.
Weiss, H. B.,	*A book about chapbooks: the people's literature of bygone times.* (Facsimile reprint of 1942 ed.) Hatboro, Pennsylvania Folklore Association, 1969.
Welch, D'A.,	*A bibliography of American children's books printed prior to 1821.* Worcester, Mass., American Antiquarian Society & Barre Publishers, 1972.
Welsh, C.,	*On some books for children of the last century* [etc.], 1886; *On coloured books for children.* 1887. (Nos. XI and XIII of *Opuscula*, published by The Sette of Odd Volumes, London, privately printed.)
	A bookseller of the last century: being some account of the life of John Newbery and of the books he published [etc.]. London, Griffith, Farran, Okeden & Welsh, 1885.
Yonge, C. M.,	*Children's literature of the last century.* (From *Macmillan's Magazine*, July, August and September, 1869; reprinted in *Signal*, nos. i-iii, 1970.)

Bravo-Villasante, C.,	*Historia de la literatura infantil español.* 2ed. Madrid, Doncel, 1963.
Dyrenfurth-Gräbsch, I.,	*Geschichte des deutschen Jugendbuches.* 3ed. Zürich, Atlantis, 1967.
Gumuchian & Co.,	*Les livres de l'enfance du XVe au XIXe siècle.* 2 vols. Paris, Gumuchian, 1930.
Hazard, P.,	*Les livres, les enfants et les hommes.* Paris, 1932.
	Books, children & men. 4ed. Boston, The Horn Book Inc., 1967.
Hürlimann, B.,	*Europäische Kinderbücher in drei Jahrhunderten.* 2ed. Zürich, Atlantis, 1963.
	Three centuries of children's books in Europe, translated (from the second edition) and edited by B. Alderson. London, OUP, 1967.
Landwehr, J.,	*Fable-books printed in the Low Countries : a concise bibliography until 1800.* Nieuwkoop, B. De Graaf, 1963.
Nuremberg, Stadtbibliothek,	*Bibliographie der Nürnberger Kinder- und Jugendbücher, 1522–1914.* Bamberg, Meisenbach, 1961.
Rümann, A.,	*Alte deutsche Kinderbücher.* Mit Bibliographie. Vienna, Reichner, 1937.
Simonsen, I.,	*Den danske børnebog i det 19. aarhundrede.* 2ed. Copenhagen, Nyt Nordisk Forlag: A. Busck, 1966.
Wouters, D.,	*Over het illustreren van leesboeken voor kinderen.* Bussum, C. A. J. Dishoeck, 1913.
Zweigbergk, E. von,	*Barnboken i Sverige, 1750–1950.* (English summary.) Stockholm, Rabén & Sjögren, 1965.

2 Early children's books

GENERAL BOOKS

Bilderbuch für Kinder, J. Bertuch (Weimar, 1795).

The Book of Wonders; or, Engravings and Descriptions of Some of the Most Remarkable Natural and Artificial Curiosities in the World (London, J. J. Griffin) [1850?].

The Child's Own Storybook, Mrs Jerram (2ed. London, Darton & Clark) [1840?].

The Juvenile Magazine; or, Instructive and Entertaining Miscellany for Youth of Both Sexes (London, J. Marshall & Co., 1788).

Lectures at My School; or, Playground Conversations (London, W. Darton, jun.) [c. 1830].

More Seeds of Knowledge, J. Corner (London, Dean & Munday) [1840?].

A Museum for Young Gentlemen and Ladies; or, a Private Tutor for Little Masters and Misses (8ed. London, Newbery & Carnan, 1776).

The Nursery Offering; or, Children's Gift for 1835 (Edinburgh, Waugh & Lines, 1835).

The Parent's Cabinet of Amusement and Instruction. 3 vols (London, Smith Elder & Co., 1832–35).

The Picturesque Primer; or, Useful Matter Made Pleasing Pastime for Leisure Hours, Rev. W. Fletcher (London, J. Harris) [1828].

The Prettiest Book for Children; Being the History of the Enchanted Castle, Don Stephano Bunyano (London, E. Newbery) [c. 1780?].

The Progress of Man and Society, Rev. J. Trusler (for the author, 1791).

Sir Harry Herald's Graphical Representation of the Dignitaries of England (London, J. Harris & Son, 1820).

Stories for Short Students; or, Light Lore for Little People, Rev. E. Mangin (London, J. Harris, 1829).

The Child's Primer; or, First Book for Children (York, J. Kendrew)
[*c.* 1815?].

Easy Lessons; or, Leading Strings to Knowledge (New ed. London, Grant &
Griffith, 1848).

*Familiar Dialogues for the Instruction and Amusement of Children of Four and
Five Years Old* (London, J. Marshall) [1783?].

The Infant's Toy Book of Pretty Tales (London, A. K. Newman & Co.)
[*c.* 1830].

The Infant Tutor; or, Easy Spelling Book for Little Masters and Misses
(London, Newbery & Carnan, 1769).

Instructive and Entertaining Dialogues for Children, Mrs Guppy (4ed. London,
E. Wallis, 1833).

Lessons for Children; or, Rudiments of Good Manners, Morals and Humanity,
Mrs Fenwick (London, M. J. Godwin, Juvenile Library, 1813).

Little Prattle over a Book of Prints with Easy Tales for Children (London,
W. Darton & J. Harvey, 1804).

Mama's Lessons for her Little Boys and Girls (9ed. London, Grant &
Griffith, 1846).

Mirth without Mischief (London, J. Davenport for C. Sheppard) [1780?].

*A New Lottery Book of Birds and Beasts for Children to Learn their Letters by as
Soon as they Can Speak* (Newcastle, T. Saint for W. Charnley, 1771).

Nursery Reading in Words not Exceeding Four Letters (London, E. Wallis)
[*c.* 1835?].

The Only Method to Making Reading Easy; or, Child's Best Instructor,
T. Hastie (73ed. Newcastle, E. Charnley, 1839).

*Papa's Book; Designed to Teach his Little Ones to Think, to Observe, and to
Reason*, Rev. B. H. Draper (London, Houlston & Co., 1838).

The Picturesque Primer; or, First Steps up the Ladder of Learning (London,
J. Harris, 1824).

*A Present from Windsor for Good Boys and Girls, Written in Words of One
Syllable Only*, A. Chapman (New ed. London, A. Chapman, 1825).

Reading Book, Containing Useful and Pleasing Lessons, Rev. England (3ed.
London, Murphy, 1823).

Reading Without Tears; or, a Pleasant Mode of Learning to Read (London,
Hatchards, 1869).

Richardson's British Primer; or, Young Child's First Book (Derby,
T. Richardson, 1846).

The Royal Primer; or, Easy and Pleasant Guide to the Art of Reading
(Brentford, P. Norbury) [1800?].

The Silver Primer (York, J. Kendrew) [*c.* 1815?].

Simple Stories in Words of One Syllable for Little Boys and Girls (London,
Grant & Griffith) [*c.* 1820?].

*Spring Flowers and Monthly Monitor; or, Early Lessons Adapted to Every
Season of the Year* (London, J. Harris, 1832).

*Tom Thumb's Play-Book to Teach Children their Letters by a New and Pleasant
Method* (New ed. Alnwick, W. Davison) [*c.* 1840?].

A Waggon Load of Gold for Little Masters and Misses (London, T. Batchelor)
[1810?].

Abécédaire des Petits Enfants (Geneva) [*c.* 1855].

Alphabet avec Exercises Méthodiques sur les Principales Difficultés de la Lecture
(Paris) [1865?].

Contes dans un Nouveau Genre pour les Enfants qui Commence à Lire (Paris,
 1808).
Je Saurai Lire: Alphabet Méthodique et Amusant, Par un Papa (Paris)
 [*c.* 1890?].
Lectures graduées pour les Enfants du Premier Âge, Abbé Gaultier (New ed.,
 Paris) [*c.* 1850?].
Le Premier Livre des Petits Enfants; ou, Contes d'une Mère, M. Dumont
 (Paris, A. Desesserts) [*c.* 1855?].

ABC Bilder und Lesebuch (2ed. Nuremberg, G. N. Renner) [*c.* 1845?].
*Kurze Erzählungen. . . . Ein Lehr- und Lesebuch für die deutsche Schüler in
 Bayern*, C. von Schmidt (Munich, 1866).
Martha und ihre Puppe: ein Lesebuch für kleine artige Töchter, F. L. Fischer
 (Berlin) [1861].
Perlen: kleine Erzählungen für freundliche Kinder von 5–8 Jahren, A. Stein
 (3ed. Berlin) [*c.* 1860?].

COUNTING BOOKS

*Amusing Division. Amusing Multiplication. Amusing Pence Table. Merry
 Multiplication.* All published by Dean & Son, London, *c.* 1845.

RELIGIOUS INSTRUCTION

*An Abridgement of Scripture History Designed for the Amusement and
 Improvement of Children* (London, Ryland, 1772).
*An Abridgement of the New Testament; or, the Life, Miracles and Death of Our
 Lord and Saviour Jesus Christ* (Glasgow, T. Lumsden & Son) [*c.* 1815].
*Bible Events: the Life of Our Lord Jesus Christ, illustrated with Pictures
 designed by A. Dürer* (London, J. Cundall, 1844).
Bible Quadrupeds: the Natural History of Animals Mentioned in Scripture,
 S. Williams (London, C. Tilt, 1838).
The Book of Sunday Pictures for Little Children: Moses to Sampson (London,
 Religious Tract Society) [*c.* 1850].
Child's First Tales, Chiefly in Words of One Syllable, Rev. C. Wilson. 2 vols
 (Kirkby Lonsdale, A. Foster, 1836).
A Compendious History of the Old and New Testament (9ed. London,
 T. Caslon) [*c.* 1785].
A Description of a Set of Prints Taken from the New Testament, S. Trimmer
 (London, Baldwin, Craddock & Joy, 1825).
Divine Emblems; or, Temporal Things Spiritualised for the Use of Young People,
 J. Bunyan (London, T. Bennett) [*c.* 1800?].
Earth's Many Voices (London, Society for Promoting Christian
 Knowledge, 1863).
*Fanny and her Mamma; or, Easy Reading Lessons. In which it is Attempted to
 Bring Scriptural Principles into Daily Practice* (London, Grant & Farran,
 1848).
Histories from Scripture for Children: Exemplified by Appropriate Domestic Tales,
 Miss Graham (London, Dean & Munday, 1834).
The History of Jacob: a Scripture Narrative in Verse (New ed. London,
 R. Miller) [*c.* 1820?].
The History of Joseph (London, Society for Promoting Christian
 Knowledge) [1868].
The History of the Holy Bible . . . Attempted in Easy Verse, J. Fellows. 2 vols
 (London, for Scatcherd and Letterman, 1811).

Isaac and Rebecca, C. C. Richardson (London, Darton, Harvey & Darton, 1817).

Learning to Feel (London, Religious Tract Society) [1845?].

Mamma's Bible Stories for Her Little Boys and Girls . . . Adapted to the Capacities of Very Young Children (6ed. London, Grant & Griffith, 1846).

The Modern Hieroglyphic Bible (London, R. Harrild, 1815).

A New Hieroglyphic Bible (Derby) [1825?].

The New Testament Adapted to the Capacities of Children [etc.] (London, J. Newbery, 1755).

Old Testament Stories in Rhyme Adapted for Young Persons [etc.] (London, W. Booth, 1826).

The Principal Events in the Life of Moses [etc.], H. Lacey (London, Darton, Harvey & Darton, 1815).

Scriptural Tales: the History of Samuel; or, Children may be Wise. The History of David and the Prophet Daniel, J. Corner (London, Dean & Son, 1854).

Scripture History Including the Lives of the Most Celebrated Apostles [etc.], Rev. I. B. Watkins. 2 vols (London, Jones & Co., 1823).

Sermons to Children, to Which are Added, Short Hymns Suited to the Subject (5ed. London, Philanthropic Society) [1830?].

Stories from Scripture on an Improved Plan: Old Testament, Rev. B. H. Draper (2ed. London, J. Harris) [1828?].

Stories on the Ten Commandments [etc.], F. Upcher (2ed. London, Darton & Harvey, 1841).

The Sunday Picture Book (London, Society for Promoting Christian Knowledge) [1852].

MORAL IMPROVEMENT

The Adventures of Master Headstrong and Miss Patient in their Journey towards the Land of Happiness (London, J. Bonsor) [c. 1800?].

Fables in Words of One Syllable, M. Godolphin (London, Cassell, Petter & Galpin) [1868].

The Affectionate Parent's Gift and the Good Child's Reward. . . . Poems and Essays on Natural, Moral, and Religious Subjects, H. S. Horsley. 2 vols (London, T. Kelly, 1834).

Amusing and Instructive Tales for Youth in Thirty Poems, with Moral Applications in Prose, J. H. Wynne (London, J. Harris, 1815).

Beauty but Skin Deep, M. Elliott (London, W. Darton) [c. 1820?].

Choice Emblems: Natural, Historical, Fabulous, Moral and Divine, for the Improvement of Youth (London, J. Chapman, 1785).

A Collection of Fables for the Instruction and Amusement of Little Masters and Misses (York, J. Kendrew) [c. 1825?].

Entertaining Instructions, in a series of Familiar Dialogues between a Parent and his Children, Interspersed with Original Fables [etc.] (London, for J. Hatchard, 1805).

Franklin's Way to Wealth; or, 'Poor Richard Improved', B. Franklin (London, W. & T. Darton, 1807).

Good and Bad; or, Which to Follow and What to Avoid. Related Chiefly in Monosyllables and adapted to the Infant Capacity, W. Limming (London, Dean & Munday) [c. 1850?].

Little Truths Concerning Information on Divers Subjects for the Instruction of Children. 2 vols (London, Darton & Harvey, 1800).

Maxims and Morals . . . being Incitements to Industry, Frugality and Prudence,
B. Franklin (London, Darton & Harvey, 1807).

A Mirror for the Female Sex; Historical Beauties for Young Ladies,
M. Pilkington (London, Vernor & Hood, 1798).

*Moral Instructions of a Father to his Son, Comprehending a Whole System of
Morality* (2ed. Newcastle, T. Saint, 1772).

*The Pleasing Instructor; or, Packet of Pictures for all Good Children with Prose
Explanations and Poetical Applications* (London, by and for Hodgson &
Co.) [1823?].

*Proverbs Exemplified and Illustrated by Pictures from Real Life . . . Designed
as a Succession-Book to Æsop's Fables by the Rev. J. Trusler*, 1790.

Stories by a Mother for the Use of her Own Children (London, Darton, Harvey
& Darton, 1818).

*Take Your Choice; or, the Difference Between Virtue and Vice Shown in
Opposite Characters* (London, J. Harris, 1805).

Tales for Youth in Thirty Poems . . . [with] Moral Applications (London, for
E. Newbery, 1794).

Album des Petits Garçons; ou, Delassemens du Coeur et de l'Esprit, J. Michel
(Paris, 1838).

*Contes à ma Petite Fille et à mon Petit Garçon pour les Amuser, leur Former un
Bon Coeur et les Corriger des Petits Défauts de leur Âge*, Madame Renneville
(5ed. Paris, chez Santin, 1823).

Contes Moraux pour la Jeunesse, Théophile, *pseud.* (Mayence) [*c.* 1825?].

Das Fabelbuch für Kindheit und Jugend, J. A. L. Loehr (Leipzig, 1824).

*Geschichtenbuch für die Kinderstube: kleine moralische Erzählungen für Kinder
von fünf bis acht Jahren*, H. Hoffmann (4ed. Stuttgart, 1857).

Hundertundfünfzig moralische Erzählungen für kleine Kinder, F. Hoffmann
(13ed. Stuttgart) [*c.* 1855?].

*Vernunftkatechismus; ein Geschenk für Kinder. (Principes de morale, pour les
enfants)*, F. Hermann (4ed. Leipzig) [*c.* 1815?].

HISTORY BOOKS

An Abridgement of English History from the Conquest to the Present Reign.
2 vols (London, J. Marshall, for the Juvenile or Child's Library,
1800).

Anecdotes of Kings Selected from History; or, Gertrude's Stories for Children
(London, J. Harris, 1837).

A Concise History of England Comprised in a Set of Easy Lessons, S. Trimmer.
2 vols (New ed. London, J. Harris & Son, 1823).

*Conversations and Amusing Tales offered to the Public for the Youth of Great
Britain*, H. English (for the author, 1799).

A Description of a Set of Prints of Ancient History, S. Trimmer. 2 vols
(London, J. Marshall) [*c.* 1790?].

The French History Briefly Told from Early Times to the Present Period
(London, J. Harris, 1833).

*Historical Prints Representing Some of the Most Memorable Events in English
History*, E. Taylor (London, Harvey & Darton, 1821).

A History of Germany . . . to the Year 1850 (Rev. ed. London, J. Murray,
1853).

Life of King George the 4th, W. Belch (London, W. Belch) [*c.* 1825?].

Marshall's Abridgement of English History (London, J. Marshall) [1803?].

New and Comprehensive Lessons Containing a General Outline of Antient History,
  S. Trimmer (London, J. Harris, 1828).

*A New Roman History from the Foundation of Rome to the End of the
  Commonwealth* (London, F. Newbery, 1770).

*A New Series of Prints Accompanied by Easy Lessons Containing a General
  Outline of Roman History*, S. Trimmer (London, for J. Harris, 1804).

*A Picture of the Manners, Customs, Sports and Pastimes of the Inhabitants of
  England*, J. Aspin (London, J. Harris, 1825).

Portraits and Characters of the Kings of England, 2 pts. (London, J. Harris &
  Son, 1823).

A Series of Prints Designed to Illustrate the Ancient History (Issued with:
  A Description of a Set of Prints [etc.]), S. Trimmer. 2 vols (London,
  Baldwin & Craddock, 1828).

A Short History of France, Mrs Moore. 2 vols (London, Baldwin, Craddock
  & Joy, 1819).

Stories from Roman History (London, Harvey & Darton, 1823).

Stories of the Tower, M. Wilson (3ed. London, Cassell) [*c.* 1890].

True Stories from Modern History . . . to the Battle of Waterloo. By a Mother
  (2ed. London, Harris & Son) [1826?].

True Stories from the History of Scotland (4ed. London, J. Harris, 1829).

GEOGRAPHY AND TRAVEL

Around and About Old England, C. Mateaux (London, Cassell, Petter &
  Galpin, 1877).

*The Book of the United Kingdom, written by Uncle John for his Youthful
  Friends* (London, Darton & Clark) [1839?].

Capitals of Europe (for the Booksellers) [*c.* 1840].

*Cosmorama: the Manners, Customs, and Costumes of All the Nations of the
  World*, J. Aspin (New ed. London, J. Harris, 1834).

The Countries of Europe and the Manners and Customs of its Various Nations
  (London, T. Dean & Co.) [*c.* 1825?].

The Curiosities of London and Westminster (London, E. Newbery, 1786).

*A Geographical Present; being Descriptions of the Principal Countries of the
  World*, M. A. Venning (3ed. London, Harvey & Darton, 1820).

Grandpapa Easy's Countries of Europe (London, Dean & Co.) [*c.* 1850].

The Juvenile Rambler; in a Series of Reading Lessons Designed for Children
  (London, J. Harris) [*c.* 1825?].

*The Juvenile Rambler; or, Sketches and Anecdotes of the Peoples of Various
  Countries with Views of the Principal Cities of the World* (London, J. Harris,
  1838).

Lapland Sketches (London, Harris & Son, 1822).

The Little Traveller, where he Went to and what he Saw (London, Dean &
  Co.) [*c.* 1840?].

London Town, F. Leigh (London, M. Ward, 1883).

A Month in London; or, Some of its Modern Wonders Described, J. Taylor
  (London, Harvey & Darton, 1832).

Mungo; or, the Little Traveller [*etc.*] (London, S. & A. Davis, 1818).

National Character Exhibited in Forty Geographical Rhymes, Miss O'Keefe
  (Lymington, for Darton, Harvey & Darton, 1818).

Peter Parley's Visit to London during the Coronation of Queen Victoria (London,
  C. Tilt, 1838).

The Public Buildings of London and Westminster Described, F. Shoberl
  (London, J. Harris, 1838).

Pug's Tour through Europe; or, the Travell'd Monkey (London, J. Harris &
    Son, 1824).
Reuben Ramble's Travels through the Counties of England. With Maps and
    Historical Vignettes (London, Darton & Co.) [*c.* 1850?].
*Scenes in Africa for the Amusement and Instruction of Little Tarry-at-Home
    Travellers*, Rev. I. Taylor (3ed. London, Harris & Son, 1821).
*Scenes in England for the Amusement and Instruction of Little Tarry-at-Home
    Travellers*, Rev. I. Taylor (4ed. J. Harris, 1826).
A Schoolboy's Visit to London (London, E. Wallis) [1826?].
Stories about Europe (London, Dean & Co.) [*c.* 1850].
Tales of Travel, consisting of Narratives of Various Journeys, F. B. Miller
    (London, Harvey & Darton, 1833).
The Traveller; or, Entertaining Journey round the Habitable Globe (4ed.
    London, J. Harris) [1825?].
Travels in Africa (London, C. J. G. & F. Rivington, 1831).
Various Costumes of the Habitable World (London, G. Martin) [*c.* 1815?].
Views of the Principal Buildings in London. 2 vols. (London, J. Marshall for
    the Juvenile or Child's Library, 1800).
*A Visit to London, Containing a Description of the Principal Curiosities in the
    British Metropolis* (New ed. London, Darton & Clark) [*c.* 1840?].
A Visit to Uncle William in Town [etc.] (London, J. Harris, 1818).
Wonders! Descriptive of Some of the most Remarkable of Nature and Art
    (London, J. Harris, 1821).
The Young Traveller; or, a Brief Sketch of All Nations (London, W. Darton
    & Son) [*c.* 1840?].
*The Youth's Compendium of Information on the Arts and Advances in Life and
    Society Exemplified in the Rise, Progress and Present State of the Great
    Metropolis, London* (London, Fletcher & Co.) [1835?].

Beautés de l'Histoire des Voyages en Europe. Blismon (New ed. Paris)
    [*c.* 1840?].

*Aus allen Welttheilen: Scenen und Bilder zur Unterhaltung und Belehrung für
    die reifere Jugend*, F. Hoffmann (Stuttgart, Schmidt & Spring, 1855).
*Landschafts—und Sittengemalde, Thier—u. Pflanzenbilder für die reifere Jugend
    von 10 bis 15*, R. Niedergesaess (Vienna, R. Lechner) [1865?].
Peter Parley's ausgewählte Erzählungen für die Jugend (2ed. Stuttgart,
    1850).

STREET CRIES AND OCCUPATIONS

The Adventures of a Coal-Mine, H. Harcourt (London, Westley & Davis,
    1836).
Artificiana; or, a Key to the Principal Trades (Edinburgh, Oliver & Boyd,
    1819).
The Biography of a Brown Loaf, Rev. I. Taylor (London, J. Harris, 1829).
The Book of English Trades and Library of the Useful Arts (New ed. London,
    R. Phillips, 1818).
The Book of Trades; or, Circle of the Useful Arts (Glasgow, R. Griffin & Co.,
    1835).
The Book of Trades; or, Library of the Useful Arts, 3 vols (London, Tabart &
    Co., 1804–11).
The Cries of London for the Instruction and Amusement of Good Children (York,
    J. Kendrew) [*c.* 1835].

The Farm: a New Account of Rural Toils and Produce, J. Taylor (London, J. Harris, 1832).

The History of a Cup of Tea in Rhymes and Pictures (London, Griffith & Farran) [1860].

Little Jack of All Trades (London, Darton, Harvey & Darton, 1812).

The Mine, Rev. I. Taylor (4ed. London, J. Harris, 1832).

The New Cries of London: a Pretty Present for All Good Girls and Boys (London, O. Hodgson) [*c.* 1830?].

Old English Cries with Attractions to the Notice of Children in a Set of Pictures (Chelmsford, I. Marsden) [*c.* 1815?].

Rhymes and Pictures to Illustrate the Histories of a Scuttle of Coals, a Bale of Cotton, and a Golden Sovereign, W. Newman (London, Griffith & Farran) [1860?].

Rural Employments; or, a Peep into Village Concerns Designed to Instruct the Mind of Children, M. Elliott (London, W. Darton, 1820).

The Ship: a Description of Different Kinds of Vessels . . . with the Distinctive Flags of Various Nations, Rev. I. Taylor (4ed. London, J. Harris, 1835).

Sugar: How it Grows, and How it is Made: a Pleasing Account for Young People (London, Darton & Clark) [1844?].

Galerie Industrielle; ou, Application des Produits de la Nature aux Arts et Métiers, Madame H. (Paris, 1822).

NATURAL HISTORY AND SCIENCE

General books

The Beauties of Creation; or, a New Moral System of Natural History, 5 vols (2ed. London, G. Riley, 1793).

The Boy's Summer Book; Descriptive of the Seasons, Scenery, Rural Life and Country Amusement, T. Miller (London, Chapman & Hall, 1846).

Charlie's Discoveries: a Good Use for Eyes and Ears (London, Darton & Clarke, 1846).

The Children's Picture Book of Quadrupeds and Other Mammalia (London, Sampson Low & Co., 1860).

Country Walks of a Naturalist with his Children, Rev. W. Houghton (7ed. London, Groombridge & Sons) [*c.* 1875?].

Domestic Pets, their Habits and Management. With illustrative Anecdotes, Mrs Loudon (London, Grant & Griffith, 1851).

Domestic Recreation; or, Dialogues Illustrative of Natural and Scientific Subjects, P. Wakefield (London, for Darton, Harvey & Darton, 1818).

Glimpses of Natural History (London, Harvey & Darton) [*c.* 1845?].

Glimpses of Nature and Objects of Interest Described during a Visit to the Isle of Wight, Mrs Loudon (London, Grant & Griffith, 1844).

Instinct Displayed in a Collection of Well Authenticated Facts Exemplifying the Extraordinary Sagacity of Various Species of the Animal Creation, P. Wakefield (Dublin, M. Goodwin, 1817).

Juvenile Rambles through the Paths of Nature (New ed. Swaffham, S. Skill, 1830).

Lessons of Wisdom for the Young; or, Spring Mornings and Evenings, Rev. W. Fletcher (London, J. Harris, 1828).

Mrs Trimmer's Introduction to Natural History in an Easy and Familiar Style Adapted to the Capacities of Children (London, Hamilton & Co.) [*c.* 1840?].

A Natural History of Beasts and Birds (Derby, T. Richardson) [*c.* 1830?].

A Natural History of the Most Remarkable Quadrupeds, Birds, Fishes, Serpents, Reptiles and Insects, M. Trimmer, *pseud.* (London, C. & C. Whittingham, 1825).

A Present for the Young Curious: Being a Series of Engravings of Birds, Beasts &c. explained by a Mother to her Inquisitive Family Circle (London, Harvey & Darton, 1824).

Sketches from Nature; or, Hints to Juvenile Naturalists (London, Harvey & Darton, 1830).

Sketches of Natural History, M. Howitt (London, Effingham Wilson, 1834).

Uncle Buncle's True and Instructive Stories about Animals, Insects and Plants; or, Aversion Subdued, R. Edgar (London, Dean & Munday) [1841?].

A Visit to the Zoological Gardens in Regent's Park (London, Dean & Co.) [*c.* 1845?].

The Year-Book of Natural History for Young Persons, Mrs Loudon (London, J. Murray, 1842).

Birds

Birds and Insects: Dialogues in Prose and Verse Illustrative of their Habits and Instincts, J. Bragg (London, Harvey & Darton, 1844).

The Boy and the Birds, E. Taylor (3ed. London, R. Yorke Taylor & Co., 1848).

Pretty Stories about Birds (London, Darton & Co.) [*c.* 1860?].

The Sylvan Melodist; or, a Cabinet of the More Familiar British Birds (London, W. Darton & Son) [1840?].

Tales about Birds, Illustrative of their Nature, Habits and Instincts, T. Bingley (London, C. Tilt, 1839).

Tommy Trip's Museum; or, a Peep at the Feathered Creation, 2 pts (London, J. Harris & Son) [1832?].

Uncle Buncle's New Book of Birds (London, Dean & Son) [1841?].

Winged Things; or, True Stories about Birds for Young Children (London, Seeley, Jackson & Halliday, 1849).

Flowers, Trees etc.

Conversations on Botany, Mrs Marcet (6ed. London, Longmans, 1828).

The Forest; or, Rambles in the Woodland, J. Taylor (London, Harris, 1831).

The Wonders of Trees, Plants and Shrubs, Recorded in Anecdotes, J. Taylor (London, W. Darton) [*c.* 1810].

Woodland Rambles: Uncle Ben's Conversations with his Nephews on the Beauty and Utility of English Timber Trees (London, R. Tyas, 1839).

Words by the Wayside; or, the Children and the Flowers, E. Ayton (London, Grant & Griffith, 1850).

Animals

Anecdotes of Animals (London, Harvey & Darton, 1832).

The Child's Picture Book of Domestic Animals (London, G. Routledge & Sons, 1869).

The History of Beasts in Miniature Adapted to the Juvenile Capacity (London, E. Langley) [*c.* 1805?].

Little Animals Described for Little People (London, Seeley, Jackson & Halliday, 1865).

Stories Illustrative of the Instinct of Animals, their Characters and Habits, T. Bingley (London, C. Tilt, 1838).

The Zoological Gardens (Aunt Louisa's London Toy Books) (London,
   F. Warne & Co.) [*c*. 1867?].

Insects, Reptiles etc.

Insects and Reptiles with their Uses to Man (London, Darton & Clark)
   [*c*. 1840?].
The Natural History of Reptiles and Serpents (London, W. Wetton, 1836).
A Natural History of Reptiles, Serpents and Insects (Alnwick, W. Davison)
   [1815?].
Scenes of Industry Displayed in the Bee-Hive and the Ant-Hill (2ed. London,
   J. Harris, 1830).

General science

Scientific Amusements for Young People, J. H. Pepper (London, G. Routledge
   & Sons) [1880?].
*Scientific Dialogues, Intended for the Instruction and Entertainment of Young
   People: in which First Principles of Natural and Experimental Philosophy are
   Fully Explained*, Rev. J. Joyce. 6 vols (New ed. London, Baldwin,
   Craddock & Joy, 1825).
The Story of a Tinder-Box [*etc.*] *(The Romance of Science)*, C. M. Tidy
   (London, Society for Promoting Christian Knowledge, 1889).

Les Animaux Domestiques (Paris, A. Quantin) [1885?].
Les Bêtes Chez Elles (Paris) [*c*. 1890?].
Introduction Familière à la Connaissance de la Nature. Traduction libre de
   l'Anglais [of Mrs Trimmer]. Abbé Berquin (Paris, 1802).

The French and English Pictorial Vocabulary, N. Whittock (London,
   W. Treacher & Co.) [*c. 1835?*].
Lectures pour les Enfans de Quatre Ans [1805?].

The Juvenile Grammar, J. Hutchinson (9ed. London, Wright, Simpkin &
   Co.) [1854].
*Mary's Grammar: Interspersed with Stories and Intended for the Use of
   Children*, Mrs Marcet (3ed. London, Longman, Orme, Green &
   Longmans, 1838).

A Short List of Selected Collections of Children's Books

For English language children's books, the largest collections are to be found in The British Library and the Victoria and Albert Museum in England; in Toronto Public Library in Canada; and in the American Antiquarian Society, the Library of Congress, and the Philadelphia Free Library in the USA.

For collections of children's books in other languages, the national library of the country concerned is usually the best place to start enquiries.

Europe

Great Britain

The old established copyright libraries receive a copy of all books published in Great Britain; these are The British Library, London; The University Library, Cambridge; The Bodleian Library, Oxford. The National Libraries of Scotland and Wales and Trinity College, Dublin receive copies of all books associated with their respective countries.

See also: 'Special Collections of Children's Literature in the South-East', by Lance Salway, Library Association, 1972

London Collections:
Hammersmith Public Library
Kensington & Chelsea Public Library
Renier Collection (now being transferred to the National Art Library, Victoria and Albert Museum)
Victoria and Albert Museum (National Art Library)
Wandsworth Public Library

Collections outside London:
Bedford, College of Education (Hockliffe Collection)
Birmingham, City Library (Parker Collection)
Edinburgh, Museum of Childhood
Manchester, School of Librarianship
Norwich, Bridewell Museum
Preston, Harris Public Library (Spencer Collection)

Austria
Internationales Institut für Kinder-, Jugend-, und Volksliteratur.

Denmark
Statens Paedagogiske Studiensamling

German Democratic Republic
Kinderbuchabteilung der Deutschen Staatsbibliothek, Berlin

German Federal Republic
Institut für Jugendbuchforschung, Frankfurt a.M.
Internationale Jugendbibliothek, Munich

Holland
Bureau Boek en Jeugd der c.v., The Hague

Russia
Dom Detskoi Knigi, Moscow (House of Children's Books)

Sweden
Barnboksinstitutet, Stockholm

Switzerland
Johanna Spyri Archiv, Zurich
Schweizerisches Jugendbuch-Institut, Zurich

United States of America and Canada

USA
See: 'Subject collections in children's literature', Edited by C. W. Field (New York and London, 1969)
This contains a *Directory of Collections*. Among the main collections listed are:
Chicago, Center for Children's Books
Minneapolis, University of Minnesota
New York, Columbia University (including Teachers' College)
New York, Public Library
New York, Pierpont Morgan Library
Philadelphia, Free Library (including Rosenbach Collection)
Washington, Library of Congress (Children's Book Section)
Worcester, American Antiquarian Society (including D'Alté Welch Collection)

Canada
Toronto, Public Library (Boys' and Girls' House)

List of Plates

1 *The Pilgrims: or, First Settlers of New England*. Baltimore, 1825
2 *Divine and Moral Songs for Children* by Isaac Watts. Worcester, Mass., 1788
3 *The Most Surprising Adventures and Wonderful Life of Robinson Crusoe, of York, Mariner* by D. Defoe. Portland, 1789
4 *Alice's Adventures in Wonderland* by Lewis Carroll. 1866
5 *A Little Pretty Pocket-Book, Intended for the Instruction and Amusement of Little Master Tommy and Pretty Miss Polly* [etc.]. Worcester, Mass., 1787
6 *The History of Goody Two-Shoes* [etc.]. 1793
7 *German Popular Stories*. Collected by M. M. Grimm, from oral tradition. 1823
8 *History of British Birds*. Newcastle, 1797
9 *Traditional Nursery Songs of England* edited by Felix Summerly. 1846
10 *A Book of Nonsense* by Edward Lear. *c.* 1870?
11 *The Alphabet of Old Friends*. 1874
12 *Hornbook*. Late eighteenth or early nineteenth century
13 *The Silver Penny for the Amusement and Instruction of Good Children*. York, *c.* 1820
14 *The Farmyard Alphabet*. *c.* 1870?
15 *Railway Alphabet*. 1852
16 *Battledore*. Philadelphia, *c.* 1817
17 *The Child's Own Battledoor*. 1798
18 *The Child's Instructor; or, Picture Alphabet*. Glasgow, *c.* 1820
19 *An Alphabet and Reading Book*. Late eighteenth century?
20 *The Silver Toy* [etc.]. Wellington, before 1828
21 *A New Lottery Book on a Plan Entirely New Designed to Allure Little Ones into a Knowledge of their Letters &c by Way of Diversion*. Edinburgh, 1819
22 *The Silver Penny* [etc.] by J. Horner. New Haven, 1805
23 *Green's Nursery Leading Strings: The Alphabet. c.* 1850?
24 *Alphabet of Nouns*. 1852
25 *A Apple Pie* by Kate Greenaway. 1886
26 *ABC du Premier Âge*. Paris, 1886
27 *The Infant's Friend; or, Easy Reading Lessons for Young Children* by a Lady. 1824
28 *ABC und Lese-Buch*. Berlin, 1846
29 *One, Two, Buckle my Shoe. c.* 1873
30 *New Stories About the Alphabet. c.* 1850
31 *The Alphabet of Nations*. 1857
32 *The New-England Primer Improved* [etc.]. Boston, 1762
33 *Leçons pour les Enfans de Trois à Huit Ans* par Mistriss Barbauld. Paris, 1817
34 *Cobwebs to Catch Flies* by Lady Fenn. 1783
35 *Cobwebs to Catch Flies* by Lady Fenn. 1783
36 *Youth's Best Friend*. Deal, 1829
37 *Alphabet Illustré*. Tours, 1867
38 *The English Spelling Book* by William Mavor. 1885
39 *The Man's Boot, and Other Tales*. 1876
40 *Marmaduke Multiply's Merry Method of Making Minor Mathematicians*. 1817
41 *Prittle Prattle's Clock. c.* 1850?
42 *Amusing Subtraction. c.* 1850
43 *Jacko's Merry Method of Learning the Pence Table. c.* 1850
44 *Das Ganze Einmaleins in Lustigen Reimen und Bildern*. Stuttgart, 1872?
45 *Amusing Addition. c.* 1850
46 *Historie de l'Ancien et du Nouveau Testament* [etc.]. Paris, 1771
47 *The History of the Holy Jesus*. Boston, 1749
48 *A Pictorial Catechism*. Paris and London, 1861
49 *A Curious Hieroglyphick Bible*, 1783
50 *Life of Our Lord*. 1866
51 *The Childhood of Christ*. 1872?

Index of Publishers

The publishers listed here are those whose publications are discussed in the text or in the captions to the plates. The index does not include books listed in any of the bibliographies. The form of the publisher's name and address is that shown in the imprint of the works listed below that name and address; it is not necessarily that of the first edition of a work.

Where more than one work appears under a publisher, they appear in *chronological order*.

ADLARD, J., London, 39, Duke Street, Smithfield,
The Young Moralist [etc.] (G. Wright). 4ed. 1792
ARLISS, John, London, 38, Newgate Street (The Juvenile Library),
The Trial of Harry Hardheart for Ingratitude and Cruelty to Certain Individuals of the Brute Creation. [c. 1820]
ASH & MASON, Philadelphia,
The Pilgrims; or, First Settlers of New England. 1825

BALDWIN & CRADOCK, London,
La Bagatelle [etc.] (N.L.). New ed. 2 vols in 1. 1829
BALDWYN, C., London, Newgate Street,
German Popular Stories (J. L. C. & W. C. Grimm). 1823–26
BASSAM, R., London,
Billy Lovegood's History of Birds and Beasts. [1795?]
BEDELET, A., Paris, rue Paree St André 14,
Grammaire Drôlatique [etc.] (M. Hamley). [c. 1865?]
BELCH, W., London, Boro',
Belch's Life of William the 4th. [1830?]
BETTESWORTH, A. and BATLEY, J., London, at the Red-Lion in Paternoster Row; at the Dove in Paternoster Row,
Youth's Divine Pastime, pt. II (R. Burton). 4ed. 1729
BOHN, H. G., London,
A History of Wonderful Inventions. 1849
BOUVIER, John, for JOHNSON & WARNER, Philadelphia,
The Cries of Philadelphia. 1810
BROWN, J. & C., London, Ave Maria Lane,
Birds, Bees and Blossoms: Original Poems for Children (T. Miller). 1858
BUSHELL, J. and GREEN, J., Boston, USA,
The History of the Holy Jesus. 6ed. 1749

CARNAN, T., London, 65, St Paul's Churchyard (see also CARNAN and NEWBERY),
The Lilliputian Auction (C. Chatter). 1777
Tea-Table Dialogues between a Governess and Mary Sensible [etc.]. 1779
CARNAN and NEWBERY, London, 65 St Paul's Churchyard,
The Holy Bible Abridged. 1770
CASSELL, PETTER and GALPIN, London, La Belle Sauvage Yard,
The Picture History of England [etc.] (Cassell's Family Picture Book). 1861
Famous Events in World History [etc.]. [1865]
CAW and ELDER, Edinburgh, High Street,
A New Lottery Book [etc.]. 1819
CHAPMAN and HALL, London,
The Juvenile Pianist; or, a Mirror of Music for Infant Minds (A. Rodwell). 1836

COOKE, I. and Co., N. Haven,
Biographical Memoirs of the Illustrious General George Washington [etc.]. (J. Corry). 1810
COOKE, Oliver D., Hartford, Conn.,
Pictures of Bible History [etc.]. 1820
CUNDALL, Joseph, London, 12 Old Bond Street,
Felix Summerly's Treasury of Pleasure Books for Children. 1841–
Traditional Nursery Songs of England. 2ed. 1846
CURTIS, John, Philadelphia, North 4th Street, no 43,
Twelve Cents Worth of Wit; or, Little Stories for Little Folk of All Denominations. [c. 1795]

DARTON, William, London, 58 Holborn Hill,
The Little Tradesman; or, a Peep into English Industry. (1824)
DARTON, William, jun., London, 58 Holborn Hill,
On the Education of Daughters (F. de S. de la M. Fénélon). 1812
Aunt Mary's New Year's Gift to Good Little Boys and Girls. 1819
London Melodies. (1812)
DARTON and Co. (DARTON and Son), London, Holborn Hill,
Green's Nursery Leading Strings: the Alphabet [etc.]. [c. 1850]
The Young Traveller; or, a Brief Sketch of All Nations. [c. 1850]
The House that Paxton Built. [1851]
DARTON and CLARK, London, Holborn Hill,
The Juvenile Naturalist; or, Walks in Spring, Summer, Autumn and Winter (Rev. B. H. Draper). 2 vols. 1839
Fireside Philosophy; or, Home Science (W. Martin). [c. 1845]
DARTON and HARVEY, London, Gracechurch Street (see also HARVEY and DARTON),
The History of Goody Two-Shoes. 1793
The Child's Own Battledoor. 1798
Footsteps to the Natural History of Birds and Beasts. 1803
Tea-Table Dialogues between a Governess and Mary Sensible [etc.] 1806
Rural Scenes; or, a Peep into the Country [etc.] (J. and A. Taylor). 1806
Rudiments of Conchology. New ed. 1837
DEAN and Co., London, Threadneedle Street,
Grandmama Easy's Account of the Public Buildings of London. [c. 1845]
Pretty Stories about the Camel. [c. 1845]
Amusing Addition. [c. 1850]
Jacko's Merry Method of Learning the Pence Table. [c. 1850]
New Stories about the Alphabet. [c. 1850]
DEAN, T. and Son, London, Threadneedle Street,
Little Tales for the Nursery. [1848?]
Amusing Subtraction. [c. 1850]
The Fine Crystal Palace the Prince Built. [1851]
Alphabet of Nouns. [1852]
Aunt Busy Bee's New London Cries. [1852]
The First Music Book; or, Gamut and Time-Table in Verse (C. Finch). [1852]
Railway Alphabet. [1852]
The Play Grammar; or, the Elements of Grammar Explained in Easy Games (J. Corner). 9ed. [c. 1855]
The Toy Grammar; or, Learning without Labour (Merriment Series; Sister Lady-Bird Series) [c. 1855?]
DEAN, T. and Son, London, 31, Ludgate Hill,
Three Useful Giants: Wind, Water, and Steam, and What They Do for Us. [c. 1850?]

DEAN and MUNDAY, London,
The Parent's Offering to a Good Child (Mrs Meeke). [*c.* 1827]
DIDIER and TEBETT, London, 75, St James Street,
Les Hochets Moraux; ou, Contes pour la Première Enfance (Monget). 1806
DUNCAN, James, Glasgow, Salt Mercat,
Guide for the Child and Youth. 1750

ELDER, —, see CAW and ELDER
ESTES and LAURIAT, Boston,
Young Folks History of the Civil War (C. E. Cheyney). 1884
EYMERY, A., Paris, rue Mazarin no. 30,
Leçons pour les Enfans (A. L. Barbauld). 1817
Petite École des Arts et Métiers (M. Jauffret). 1816

FAIRBANKS and PALMER, Chicago,
All Aboard for the Lakes and Mountains: a Trip to Picturesque Localities in the United States (E. A. Rand). 1885

GINN and Co., Boston,
Stories from English History from Earliest Times to the Present Day (A. F. Blaisdell). 1897
GREEN, J., see BUSHELL, J. and GREEN, J.
GRIFFITH and FARRAN, London, West corner of St Paul's Churchyard,
Might not Right; or, Stories of the Discovery and Conquest of America. 1858
Der Schwätzer [etc.]. 1858
The Fairy Tales of Science: a Book for Youth (J. C. Brough). 1859
The History of a Scuttle of Coals [etc.] (W. Newman). [1860]
The Man's Boot [etc.]. 1876
GRIMALDI, Stacey, London,
The Toilet. 1821
A Suit of Armour for Youth. 1824
GROOMBRIDGE and Son, London,
Seaside Walks of a Naturalist with his Children (Rev. W. Houghton). New ed. 1889

HARRIS, John, London, St Paul's Churchyard,
The Geographical Guide: a Poetical Nautical Trip [etc.]. 1805
New and Comprehensive Lessons Containing a General Outline of the New Testament (S. Trimmer). [1821?]
The Infant's Friend [etc.]. 1824
Northern Regions; or, a Relation of Uncle Richard's Voyages for the Discovery of a North West Passage. 1825
The County Album; Containing . . . Topographical Hieroglyphics [etc.]. 1829
The Wars of the Jews as Related by Josephus. 4ed. 1832
Le Babillard [etc.] (J. G. de la Voye). 2ed. 1834
The Little Botanist [etc.] (C. Halstead). 1835. (One of 'The Little Library')
HARRIS, John, and Son, London, Corner of St Paul's Churchyard,
Marmaduke Multiply's Merry Method of Making Minor Mathematicians. [1817]
Scenes in America for . . . little Tarry-at-home Travellers (Rev. I. Taylor). 1821
Scenes of British Wealth [etc.] (Rev. I. Taylor). 1823
The Infant's Grammar; or, a Pic-nic Party of the Parts of Speech. 1824
Punctuation Personified; or, Pointing Made Easy (Mr Stops). 1824
The Little Grammarian; or, An Easy Guide to the Parts of Speech (Rev. W. Fletcher). 1828
HARVEY and DARTON, London, Gracechurch Street (see also DARTON and HARVEY),
Jack of All Trades. 1806
City Scenes; or, a Peep into London for Children (J. and A. Taylor). 1828; another edition. [*c.* 1845?]
The Pictorial Grammar (A. Crowquill). 1842

Sketches from Nature; or, Hints to Juvenile Naturalists. 1830
Birds and Insects: Dialogues in Prose and Verse Illustrative of their Habits and Instincts (J. Bragg). (1844)
Glimpses of the Wonderful (A Christmas annual). 1845
HATCHARD, J., and Son, London,
Entertaining Instructions in a Series of Familiar Dialogues [etc.]. 1805
New and Comprehensive Lessons Containing a General Outline of the New Testament (S. Trimmer). [1821?]
HATCHARD and Co., London, 187, Piccadilly,
Peep of Day. Rev. ed. 1868
HAYWARD, T., Deal,
Youth's Best Friend [etc.]. New ed. 1829
HEPTINSTALL, T., London,
The Pilgrim's Progress [etc.] (J. Bunyan). 1796
HERISSANT, J. T., Paris,
Histoire de l'Ancien et du Nouveau Testament. 1771
HODGSON, Sol., for BEILBY and BEWICK, Newcastle,
History of British Birds (T. Bewick). 1797
HODGSON, T., London, in George's Court, St John's-Lane, Clerkenwell,
A Curious Hieroglyphick Bible. 1783
HOULSTON, F., and Son, Wellington,
The Moving Market; or, Cries of London [etc.]. [*c.* 1820?]
The Silver Toy [etc.]. [before 1828]
HOULSTON and STONEMAN, London,
Little Henry's Holiday at the Great Exhibition. [1851]

JANET, L., Paris, 59 rue Saint Jacques (also Mme Veuve L. Janet),
Les Petits Habitants des Fleurs. (L. Leneveux) [*c.* 1845]
Les Fleurs Parlantes. [1848]
JERRARD and Son, London,
Entomology in Sport [etc.] (Hon. Mrs W. and Lady M.). [1859]
JOHNSON, B., Philadelphia, no 31, Market Street,
Hymns in Prose for Children (A. L. Barbauld). 1806
Battledore. [*c.* 1817]

KENDREW, J., York,
The Silver Penny [etc.]. [*c.* 1820]
The Cries of York [etc.]. [1826?]
KEY and MIELKE, Philadelphia,
The Life and Adventures of Robinson Crusoe (D. Defoe). 1831
KNEELAND, S., Boston,
The New-England Primer Improved. 1762
KNIGHT, C. and Co., London,
The New Chapter of Kings; or, the History of England [etc.]. 1843
KURZBECK, Joseph Edlen von, Vienna,
Sechzig eröfnete Werkstätte [etc.]. 1789

LANE, W., London, Leadenhall Street,
Reading Made Perfectly Easy [etc.] (T. Dyke). 29ed. (1785)
LAURIAT, —, see ESTES and LAURIAT
LEACROFT, S., London, at the Globe, Charing Cross,
Orbis Sensualium Pictus . . . Joh. Amos. Comenius's Visible World [etc.] (C. Hoole). 1777
LEHUBY, P. C., Paris,
Les Jeunes Voyageurs en France [etc.] (Mme de Flesselles). 3ed. 1834
Petite Bibliothèque des Chroniques de l'Histoire de France [etc.] (A. Mazure). 2ed. (1842)
LE PRIEUR, Paris, rue des Noyers, no. 45,
La Morale Enseignée par l'Example [etc.]. 5ed. 1810
LEVRAULT, Vᵉ, Strasbourg, rue des Juifs 33,
Une Famille de Rouges-Gorges (S. Trimmer). 1847
LOCKWOOD and Co., London, 7, Stationer's Hall Court,
La Bagatelle [etc.] (L.N.). New ed. 1871

LONGMAN, T., and others, London, Paternoster Row,
Fabulous Histories; Designed for the Instruction of Children [etc.].
1786
LUCAS, F., jr., Baltimore
The Pilgrims; or, First Settlers of New England. 1825
LUMSDEN and Son, Glasgow,
The Child's Instructor; or, Picture Alphabet. [c. 1810]

MACMILLAN and Co.
Alice's Adventures in Wonderland (L. Carroll). 1866; another
edition. 1870
MAME, A. et Fils, Tours,
Alphabet Illustré. 1867
MARSHALL, John, London, no. 4 Aldermary Churchyard;
after 1787 at 17 Queen Street, Cheapside
Cobwebs to Catch Flies (Lady E. Fenn). [1783]
Fables in Monosyllables [etc.] (Mrs Teachwell). (1783)
Morals to a Set of Fables [etc.] (Mrs Teachwell) (1783)
Jemima Placid; or, the Advantages of Good Nature [etc.] (M. J.
Kilner). 3ed. 1786
A Series of Prints of Roman History (S. Trimmer). 1789 (Address
given as 4 Aldermary Churchyard)
A Concise Abridgement of Natural History. 5 vols. (The Juvenile
or Child's Library). (1800)
Captain Cook's Voyage to the Pacific Ocean. (The Juvenile or
Child's Library). (1800)
MASON, —, see ASH & MASON
MIELKE, —, see KEY and MIELKE
MOGG, W., London, 62, High Street, Bloomsbury,
The English Struwwelpeter [etc.] (H. Hoffmann). [1865?]
MONSON and Co., New-Haven,
Historical Scenes in the United States (J. W. Barber). 1827
MORGAN, W. H., Philadelphia,
The Wonderful Exploit of Guy, Earl of Warwick [c. 1830]
MOZLEY and Co., Gainsborough, Lilliputian Book Manu-
factory,
The Jack-of-All-Trades; or, the Merry, Merry Cries of London.
1794
MUNDAY, T., London, 9, Fore Street (see also DEAN and
MUNDAY),
Prittle Prattle's Clock. [c. 1850?]
MURRAY, John, London, Albemarle Street,
Little Arthur's History of England (Lady M. Callcott). 1835
A History of England (Mrs Markham). 1857
Hymns in Prose for Children (A. L. Barbauld). 1865

NEWBERY, E., London, Corner of St Paul's Churchyard,
The Brother's Gift; or, the Naughty Girl Reformed. 1773
The Blossoms of Morality. 1789; another edition. 1796
Dramatic Dialogues for the Use of Young Persons (Mrs Pinchard).
2 vols. 1792
Triumph of Good Nature [etc.]. [1801]
NEWBERY, Francis, 20, The corner of St Paul's Church-yard,
*A New Roman History from the Foundation of Rome to the End of the
Commonwealth.* 1770
NEWBERY, John, London, St Paul's Churchyard,
A Little Pretty Pocket Book [etc.]. 1744
Six Pennyworth of Wit [etc.]. [c. 1795?]
NEWMAN, A. K. and Co., London, Leadenhall Street,
The Elements of Geography. [c. 1820]
The Gamut and Time-Table in Verse [etc.] (C. Finch). [1820?]
NIMMO, W. P., Edinburgh,
King Alfred and Othere, the Discoverer of the North Cape (H. W.
Longfellow) (Marcus Ward's Royal Illuminated Legends).
[1872]
NORBURY, P., Brentford,
The Royal Primer [etc.]. 1800?

OGILVY and SPEARE, London, Middle-Row, Holborn,
The Newtonian System of Philosophy [etc.] (T. Telescope, revised
by W. Magnet). 1794
ORTON and HAWKES SMITH, Birmingham,
*The French Present; or, Easy Dialogues, French and English,
Adapted to the Capacities of Young Beginners.* 1813

PALMER, —, see FAIRBANKS and PALMER
PARK, A., London, 47, Leonard Street, Finsbury Circus,
Papa's Tales about the Sun and Stars. [c. 1845]
PARKER, John W., London, West Strand,
Pretty Lessons in Verse for Good Children [etc.] (S. Coleridge).
3ed. 1839
PHILP, John,
A Pictorial Catechism [etc.] (Rev. M. B. Couissinier). (1861)
PLON, E., NOURRIT et Cie, Paris,
Jeanne d'Arc (M. Boutet de Monvel). [1896]
PLOWMAN, T. L., Philadelphia,
Captain Smith and Princess Pocahontas (J. Davis). 1805

QUANTIN, A., Paris, 17, rue Saint Benoit,
ABC du Premier Âge. [1886]

RELIGIOUS TRACT SOCIETY, London,
Palestine for the Young. 1865
Sunday Afternooons with Mamma. 1866
RICHARDS, Grant, London, 9, Henrietta Street
The Book of Shops (E. V. Lucas). [1899]
RIVINGTON, J., and others, London,
The London Vocabulary: English and Latin. 16ed. 1771
ROBERTSON, J. and M., Glasgow,
The Natural History of Four Footed Beasts (T. Trip). 1802
ROBINSON, G. G. and J., London,
A Compendious History of England [etc.]. 1794
ROGERS, R., Newmarket,
Les Jeux de la Jeunesse; ou, Nouvelle Methode à Instruire les Enfans
[etc.]. 1814
ROUTLEDGE and Co., London,
The Little Minxes. [c. 1857]
The Young Ragamuffins. [c. 1857]
ROUTLEDGE, George, and Sons, London, Broadway, Ludgate
Hill,
Alphabet of Flowers. [1850]
Life of Our Lord. (Routledge's Large Toy Books) [1866]
The Child's Coloured Scripture Book . . . The History of Joseph.
[1867?]
Grammar in Rhyme. [1868]
Pictures of English History: from the Druids to Magna Carta. (New
Series of Shilling Toy Books). [1868]
The Purgatory of Peter the Cruel (J. Greenwood). 1868
The Child's Picture Book of Domestic Animals. 1869
The Farmyard Alphabet. [c. 1870?]
My Mother's Picture Book. [1870]
The Shilling Alphabet: Trades of London. [c. 1870?]
One, Two, Buckle my Shoe. [1873]
The Alphabet of Old Friends. [1874]
The English Spelling Book (W. Mavor). 1885
A Apple Pie (Illus. K. Greenaway). [1886]

SAMPSON LOW, Son, and MARSTON,
Divine and Moral Songs for Children (Rev. I. Watts). 1866
SCHULGEN, A. W., Paris,
A Pictorial Catechism [etc.] (Rev. M. B. Couissinier). (1861)
SCHWEITZER, Henrich, Philadelphia, an Eck der Rees un
Viertn Strasse,
*Zween Bettelknaben: eine lehrreiche Geschichte fur unsere deutschen
Kinder* [etc.]. 1806
SEELEY, JACKSON and HALLIDAY, London, Fleet Street,
Sunday Afternoons in the Nursery (M. L. Charlesworth). 1866

What Makes me Grow? Walks and Talks with Amy Dudley. 1875

SHARPE and HAILES, London,
   Sir Hornbook; or, Childe Lancelot's Expedition. A Grammatico-Allegorical Ballad. (T. L. Peacock). 1814

SIDNEY'S PRESS, New-Haven,
   Silver Penny; or, New Lottery Book for Children. (J. Horner) 1805

SIMPKIN, MARSHALL and Co., London, Stationers' Hall Court,
   Peter Parley's Tales about China and the Chinese. 1843

SMITH, W., London, 113, Fleet Street,
   True Tales of the Olden Time, Selected from Froissart (R. M. Evans). 2ed. 1842
   The Young Naturalist's Journey [etc.] (Mrs Loudon). 1840

SOCIETY FOR PROMOTING CHRISTIAN KNOW-LEDGE, London,
   The People of Europe. (Two series in one vol.). [1861–62]
   Buttercups and Daisies and Other Pretty Flowers. [c. 1870]
   Art Pictures from the Old Testament. 1894

SPEARE, —, see OGILVY and SPEARE

STANFORD, Edward, London,
   The New Picture Book, being Pictorial Lessons on Form [etc.] (N. Bohny). 8ed. [c. 1880]

TEGG, T. and Son, London, Cheapside,
   Peter Parley's Tales about the Sea and Islands in the Pacific Ocean. 3ed. 1838
   Peter Parley's Tales about the Sun, Moon and Stars. 3ed. 1838

TEGG, William, London, 85, Queen Street, Cheapside,
   The Overland Alphabet (Isabel D-). [1853]
   The Alphabet of Nations. [1857]

THIENEMANN, K., Stuttgart,
   Das Ganze Einmaleins [etc.]. [1872?]

THOMAS, Isaiah, Worcester, Mass.,
   Little Pretty Pocket Book [etc.]. 1787
   Divine and Moral Songs for Children (Rev. I. Watts). 1788

VERNOR and HOOD, London,
   The Beauties of History [etc.] (W. Dodd). 3ed. 1800

WAIT, Thomas B., Portland, Maine,
   The Most Surprising Adventures . . . of Robinson Crusoe [etc.] (D. Defoe). 1789

WARD, M. and Co., London, Chandos Street, W.C.,
   Aunt Charlotte's Stories of English History for the Little Ones (C. M. Yonge). (1873)

WARNE, Frederick and Co., London,
   Book of Nonsense (E. Lear). [c. 1870]
   The Zoological Gardens: the Lion, Tiger [etc.]. (Aunt Louisa's London Toy Books). [c. 1870]
   The Childhood of Christ. (Aunt Louisa's Sunday Books). [1872?]

WEIDMANNSCHE BUCHHANDLUNG, Berlin,
   Was Willst du Werden? 2ed. [1864?]

WESTLEY, Francis, London, 10, Stationer's Court,
   Bunyan Explained to a Child, pt. I (Rev. I. Taylor). 2ed. 1825

WHITTINGHAM and ARLISS, London, Paternoster Row,
   Memoirs of Dick, the Little Pony, Intended for the Instruction and Amusement of Little Masters and Misses. 1816

WHYTE, William, Edinburgh,
   Holiday House (C. Sinclair). 1839

WINCKELMANN und Söhne, Berlin,
   ABC und Lese-Buch. 3ed. 1846
   Teutonia: Deutschlands wichtigste Ereignisse [etc.] (E. Maukisch). 3ed. [c. 1850]

WOOD and CUNNINGHAM, Bath,
   The Beauties of Natural History Adapted to the Minds of Both Sexes [etc.]. [1777?]

WRIGHT, G., London,
   The Father of his Country; or, the History of . . . Peter the Great [etc.]. (W. H. Dilworth). 1758

General Index

This is an index of titles, writers, artists, printers, and such subjects as are not covered by the list of contents. The dates of the works as shown in this index are those of the book discussed or illustrated, and not necessarily those of first editions. Books which appear in the bibliographies are not included.

Where more than one work is shown under any heading, the order is alphabetical. Reference is also made to individual works in the index of publishers.

Numbers in italics refer to illustrations or captions.